UnConformed
BRIAN HORVATH

UnConformed
BRIAN HORVATH

UnConformed
by Brian Horvath, MA.

ISBN: 978-1-7950-7901-3

Table of Contents

Special Thanks
Foreword
Preface

PART I
INTRODUCTION

Chapter 1	My Conformed Years	**1**
Chapter 2	I Am Who I Am!	**9**
Chapter 3	Being Intentional	**15**

PART II
1 TIMOTHY BREAKDOWN

Chapter 4	What Do They Say About You?	**23**
Chapter 5	She Belongs to the Lord	**31**
Chapter 6	Mental Vigilance	**43**
Chapter 7	Relax, Dude.	**48**
Chapter 8	*Be* Respect	**52**
Chapter 9	Love Your Neighbor Selflessly	**61**
Chapter 10	Teaching Without a Degree	**67**
Chapter 11	Being Sober Matters	**75**
Chapter 12	You Don't Have to Argue	**83**
Chapter 13	Rich in Christ	**91**

PART III
MOVING FORWARD

Chapter 14	So Now What?	**98**
Chapter 15	Taking Action	**108**
Chapter 16	Living His Purpose	**113**
Chapter 17	You Are His VIP	**118**
Appendix A	A Message to Garcia	**122**
Appendix B	Links and Citations	**128**
Appendix C	Questions for Reflection	**129**

SPECIAL THANKS

Where does one even start to say, "Thank you" without causing offense to those who may have been left out?

Thank you to my parents for their continued love and providence over the first forty years of life. (That goes for the rest of my family, too.)

I was humbled by the ten or so students who bravely volunteered to read my first manuscript and were willing to provide honest feedback. Delainie Wheeler receives a special thanks because even after she viciously edited (during her summer break!) the first manuscript, she still encouraged me to continue working towards an end product. I have never seen so much red ink! If you don't know who she is yet, you will: She's a world influencer in the making. Get it done, D!

To the hundreds of students, athletes, and coaches who over the years have pushed me to hold myself accountable to the high expectations I carried, thank you. Every day you looked at not only what I said but how I did what I did. You asked tough questions that others would not and expected me to set the example. You know who you are!

When I was a high school student I would visit my brother at Concordia University in Wisconsin during Easter break. My brother introduced me to a group of men who to this day provide one of the strongest demonstrations of godly leadership I have seen. I think of them often even though they are unaware of their daily influence. Thank you for your leadership and influence. Your godly example is profound.

To the very small handful of friends who are my brothers from different mothers. Your fellowship and brotherhood has been appreciated more than you could possibly fathom. Thank you not only for the love and long conversations about anything and everything-but just your presence.

And of course, a special thanks to my brother. He has been the most stable and consistent male influence in my lifetime. Words cannot paint the level of appreciation I have for his influence, fellowship and brotherhood. He is also the editor of this book. So, thanks?

To my wife Kara, thank you. It is impossible for me to read Proverbs 31 and not think of you when it describes a woman of noble character:

> She is clothed with strength and dignity; she can laugh at the days to come. She speaks with wisdom, and faithful instruction is on her tongue. She watches over the affairs of her household and does not eat the bread of idleness. Her children arise and call her blessed; her husband also, and he praises her: Many women do noble things, but you surpass them all. Charm is deceptive, and beauty is fleeting; but a woman who fears the LORD is to be praised. Honor her for all that her hands have done, and let her works bring her praise at the city gate.

But by the grace of God and his Cross, demonstrated and manifested through you daily, I would not be who I am today. Thank you.

FOREWORD

I needed to read these words. And I am so thankful to know the man who penned them.

Brian Horvath and I have been friends for 10 years and counting. I was a confused, passionate, wide-eyed senior high school student looking for meaning and purpose. Brian was a slightly less-confused, wise and passionate high school theology teacher struggling to manifest his own meaning and purpose.

At the time, we were both wounded soldiers when we met back in the fall of 2008. I was searching for belonging, identity and security after several years of floundering about as a teenager. Brian had just come out of a few soul-crushing years of teaching, needing encouragement and hope. We got to know one another over intense chess matches and even more intense conversations.

I distinctly remember riffing on and on about John Eldredge, Iron Maiden, college, girls and Jesus. We talked *a lot* about John Eldredge and Jesus. I distinctly remember three ways that Brian responded to me and related with me during our formative year together:

He listened to me.
He loved me amid my mess.
He led me to the feet of Jesus.

For a young man in desperate need of direction and guidance, his mentorship was medicine for my wayward soul.

I love this man. I am thankful for his friendship, his leadership, and this book you now hold in your hands. It was written for such a time as this. You and I both know the battle that continues to rage among and within. The devil, that ancient accuser, liar and deceiver, wants us dead, destroyed and devastated. Our sinful nature, that old man or woman that clings so closely to our beloved and blood-bought bodies, continues to taunt, twist and terrorize us.

The world, as beautiful and beloved as she is, seeks her own pleasure and continues to rebel against her Creator and Savior. These reasons (and many more) are why this book is important — dare I say — vital. We (and I am including myself in the mix) struggle mightily to be followers of Jesus in our culture. Brian helps to shed light on why this is and what to do about it.

Like a skilled architect, he lays out the blueprint of our souls and gives us resources and tools to navigate this valley of shadows. He shows us, from the Word of God, how to be godly men and women in an age and culture that is confused as to what those terms even mean. With conviction, passion, and gentle love, Brian calls us out (himself included) and invites us to sit with Jesus — to learn from him and imitate His life.

Read *UnConformed*, letting the truth contained within, challenge, disrupt, encourage, equip and move you to the cross of Christ. Pause after each chapter, inviting Jesus into each arena of life that Brian unpacks and unveils. Most of all, rest at the foot of the cross and reflect on what our Savior has done for us. He has removed anything and everything that could possibly separate us from the eternal embrace of our Father.

He has equipped and empowered you with His Life-Giving Spirit to direct, guide and lead you as you navigate through this life. Jesus is with you! He goes before, stands beside and protects you from behind. He holds fast to you both now and forever. He is working to conform, form, and transform you more into His likeness. This is a life-long journey! Grab a cup of coffee or tea, curl up on the couch and feast your heart and mind on *UnConformed.*

It's worth the ride.

With Love,
Nathan Spaulding
Ragamuffin Pastor in Mesa, Arizona

Preface

As a theology teacher for 12th graders, each summer means attending numerous graduation parties for my recently graduated students. At the end of the 2015 school year, I was preparing for this annual onslaught of graduation parties, contemplating what I might possibly give to them as a gift. I never like going empty handed (rude), but I also do not want to give out cash (too impersonal). I prefer to give students a book that has meaning and impact.

I have four or five books that I regularly turn to for this purpose, but there was one kind of book that I wanted most to give out, which did not seem to have been written. What I wanted was a book that would relate well to young high school men, but none of the ones I reviewed piqued my interest.

I could not find a book I wanted to give recently graduated young men, so I decided I needed to write it myself. Much of what is in this book are the examples and thoughts that I try to share each year with my students—both the young men and the young women. Thus, it is worth saying that while the book is directed primarily for young men, most of it will be applicable to young women, as well.

Unfortunately, even if young men and women wanted to live a godly life, they have no idea what that means.

It is my prayer that this book will serve to bridge that gap between desiring to live God-pleasing lives but not knowing exactly how that plays out in real life. The timing couldn't be more critical for these young people. They are quickly approaching important milestones in their lives such as marriage and having children. The Bible has practical counsel for them along with many admonitions. It is better to have this knowledge now, before the decisions are to be made, rather than later, when nothing can be done except to learn how to live with regrets.

What does a godly man or woman *look* like?

When we are talking about dating and relationships in class, we first look into what it means to be a godly woman and man. We use Proverbs 31:10ff when discussing the character of a godly woman, and 1 Timothy 3 when discussing the characteristics of a godly man.

Each year, I direct my students to create a "Top 10" list of what they want their future spouse to look like inside and (possibly) out.

After the students make their list, they are directed to the book of Proverbs and 1 Timothy 3 which is quoted below and used as the basis for the thoughts in this book:

> Here is a trustworthy saying: Whoever aspires to be an overseer desires a noble task. Now the overseer is to be above reproach, faithful to his wife, temperate, self-controlled, respectable, hospitable, able to teach, not given to drunkenness, not violent but gentle, not quarrelsome, not a lover of money. He must manage his own family well and see that his children obey him, and he must do so in a manner worthy of full respect. (If anyone does not know how to manage his own family, how can he take care of God's church?) He must not be a recent convert, or he may become conceited and fall under the same judgment as the devil. He must also have a good reputation with outsiders, so that he will not fall into disgrace and into the devil's trap.

After listing various qualifications for an overseer, the Apostle Paul writes that, "He must manage his own family well and see that his children obey him, and he must do so in a manner worthy of full respect."

What does managing his family look like? Read verses two and three and we have the answer.

In verse five, Paul wonders how the overseer will manage the church if he cannot take care of his own family. There are millions of fathers in the world today who believe they are managing their family well. Unfortunately, their example, priorities, and focus have little to do with Christ. Sure, they cite Jesus and say they believe in him, but much of what they do violates this confession. It's one thing to manage your family and protect them, but it's entirely different to intentionally lead your family to the cross.

When we have the cross front and center in our minds, the entire dynamic of the family changes because the focus has shifted. It is at the cross where we see our sin, salvation and sanctification.

This shift of focus leads the family to the cross and inevitably leads the children's children to the cross. In other words, our starting point with these questions won't only alter our relationship with our spouse, or only with our children. Even the well-being and spiritual health of our grandchildren will be impacted by whether we put Jesus at the center of family. We aren't talking about only you. We are talking about you and your influence on future generations!

It will be tempting as you read the book to come to the belief that I am judging you.

The knee-jerk feeling that judging someone is 'bad' and automatically wrong and unchristian—as if the very worst thing we could do is 'judge' someone—is a common view among Americans (Christians included) that is rooted in a misunderstanding of Matthew 7:1.

For example, I recently saw a young woman post on social media something to the effect that no one is allowed to call each other out on sins. She clearly is not familiar with Scripture.

As Christians we *are* to hold one another accountable to the Word. For example:

Brothers and sisters, *if someone is caught in a sin, you who live by the Spirit should restore that person gently*. But watch yourselves, or you also may be tempted. Carry each other's burdens, and in this way you will fulfill the law of Christ. If anyone thinks they are something when they are not, they deceive themselves (Galatians 6:1-3. Emphasis added).

That's pretty clear.

Paul's words in 1 Corinthians 5 echo what he wrote in Galatians:

> But now I am writing to you that you must not associate with anyone who claims to be a brother or sister but is sexually immoral or greedy, an idolater or slanderer, a drunkard or swindler. Do not even eat with such people. What business is it of mine to judge those outside the church? *Are you not to judge those inside?* God will judge those outside. Expel the wicked person from among you. (Emphasis added.)

That's pretty clear, too.

As Christians we *are* to hold each other's actions up to Scripture and judge whether or not we are living in the light and starting at the cross or starting with the flesh and dwelling in the darkness.

Of course, it is important to note that in the Galatians passage, Paul not only highlights the need to hold one another accountable, but also urges that one does so with gentleness and humility. There is a difference between biblical discernment and being judgmental. As the rest of the Scriptures flesh out this difference, it becomes clear that ultimately it is God's Word that is judging our actions and motivations. Fellow Christians are called to admonish each other in Christ for their benefit, not their condemnation. When they admonish, they must be careful! "Watch yourselves, or you also may be tempted."

My purpose is not to write a book about what the Bible teaches on 'judging' and 'discernment.' However, because it is so common to hear admonishments waved away so quickly as "unchristian judging," I felt it necessary to offer a few passages that show that there is much more in the Bible on the matter than 'judge not, lest ye be judged.' One of the important things often forgotten is something that I will be keeping in mind throughout this book: whatever hard thing I have to say, it is offered in love, with the hope that my admonishments will help the reader live a more godly life.

This book is meant to be an encouragement, not a verdict.

I have learned over the years as a teacher that students are less likely to listen to the content if they feel the teacher believes himself to be above the very content he is teaching. If the students find the teacher to possess a "holier than thou" attitude, they most certainly will not consider listening or applying the information.

That is why it is also important to understand that when we are "judging" we are judging the actions of a person and not the person themselves. Additionally, the basis for the judgment of those actions is not our personal opinion or secular ideas of morality, but rather God's holiness and his Word. If his holiness and his Word is the standard, it prevents us from being self-righteous, self-centered, judgmental hypocrites.

A hypocritical, "holier than thou" teacher is a teacher whom no one will listen to.

As you read this book, you will see that I illustrate some of my points by bringing up anecdotes from my own life. It should be pretty evident from them that I do not at all believe I am "holier than thou." Hopefully, by including some of my experiences, readers will be more likely to take my admonitions in the spirit they are offered: with good will and good intentions, hoping that through my words people will be built up in love.[1]

---

[1] In that same spirit, insofar as some of my experiences include other members of my family, I want it understood that I am in no way being judgmental towards them.

Through this book, I pray that you may find encouragement and guidance in Scripture. Start at the cross and stay at the cross. Allow God's Word to shape you into the new creation He has in mind for you. My prayer is that through this, you will lead yourself and your family in the right direction as a man of God.

Since I understand that young ladies may very well be reading this book, looking for an idea as to what a godly man looks like, beginning with Part II, I have included small paragraphs entitled, "What I say to young ladies." These paragraphs might also give young men a different perspective, too.

The majority of resources used related to Scripture came from either Biblegateway.com or Biblestudytools.com. I will refer to their concordances, lexicons, transliterated words, pronunciation of Greek words, and interlinear Bible's, which are linked to Strong's Concordance and the NIV and KJV version of Scripture.

PART I

Chapter 1

My Conformed Years

As I teach my students and athletes, everyone is a leader because everyone influences everyone else one way or the other. Leadership is more than a title; it is influence of others. The question then is to what extent I had a positive male, biblical, influence in my life.

It would not be fair to say I didn't have positive male leadership and examples in my life because I did. Still, with all due respect to my father, he was not always a positive influence. His marriage to my mother was encouraged by the unexpected pregnancy of my brother. Both of my parents had been born in the fifties and were the products of the sixties and seventies culture. She was sixteen at the time while my father was nineteen. When my mother was nineteen, she gave birth to me.

Their marriage was not working. My father's mother died of cancer when my brother was still an infant. As one might expect, this had a tremendous impact on my father. From my perspective, it seems that over time the death of his mother was a catalyst for much anger and bitterness. His belief in God and His provision was lost. Indeed, he once told me that belief in God was for children.

Our life experiences play a significant role in who we are and influence how we influence others. In my father's case, he had experienced some significant pain and grew up very quickly. My parents would get a divorce when I was around three years old. Now, he was the father of two children while living divorced from his wife and having lost his mother. His experiences were shaping how he would raise his own children.

In those early days, my father did what many young bachelors did: play. Like most divorced families, my time was split between parents. I spent every other weekend at his house, summers included. However, due to his lifestyle, this was time often spent at his house, but not necessarily with him.

For example, one morning my father, without explanation, drove my brother and me to the Eastside of Detroit and left us on our own in his friend's apartment. The lack of décor and food in the fridge made it obvious that whomever this apartment belonged to was also a bachelor. I remember there being a poster of a half-naked woman on the wall. There we sat alone for the day while my father was presumably golfing, gambling and drinking.

As we became older my father would leave us for longer periods of times, two or three days at a crack. As teenagers it would be possible for him to be gone for longer periods of time. Of course, when I was a teenager, you can guess that this didn't bother me too much. No parent in attendance equated to freedom. What teen does not like freedom?

Still, there comes a point where every teen wants some good advice, and in most cases a parent is the place one turns. Godly advice is even better.

Both were frequently lacking from my father. For example, one day I was talking to my father about girls and sex. This would have been a good opportunity for strong *godly* leadership from my father. Instead, I received advice that came straight out of the 'liberated' decades of the '60s and '70s. The attitudes and behaviors that I had been toying around with were ones that I knew at the time probably could not be reconciled with what God's plan for sexuality was. The very things that I knew would not please God were the ones my father affirmed.

Ironically, while his mother's death appeared to harden his heart, the death of his father and the arrival of his own grandchildren seemed to soften it. After the death of his father (my grandfather), he began to manifest his love towards us in more obvious and fatherly ways. Today, I am thankful for the relationship I have with him and his desire to be a compassionate and involved grandfather.

It's not that my father didn't love us before that, because he did and he does. His expression of that love was sometimes clouded by what I view to be pride and selfishness—the same fatal flaws I possess. I have no issues admitting it; I am a selfish person. It is only within the last ten years as a parent myself, where I have become less self-centered. But 'less self-centered' does not mean that I don't have a long way to go.

My own life experiences have left their mark on me. My quest to be a godly man means that I have to confront these selfish tendencies in myself, and more than that, conform my thoughts, attitudes, and behaviors to the standards and principles that God has revealed in the Bible (Romans 12:1-3).

If I want to do more than give good advice to my children, and want also to give godly advice, it is important that I hold my life up against the Word of God. I had to decide what kind of father I wanted to be and the direction I wanted to lead my children. I needed to ask: "Where were we going as a family and how were we going to get there?"

Experience had taught me the pros and cons of the differing parenting styles at my disposal. My mother remarried when I was about five. She married a man whose parenting style was authoritative. This was in stark contrast to my father who was a permissive parent. A permissive parent is one who allows you to do what you want with little or no consequences or guidance.

Many young men would beg to have a permissive parent, but in the long run the permissive parent fails the best interest of the child. Allowed to run free without consequences, the child can quickly find themselves in all types of trouble—with themselves, and the law! Unfortunately, our culture has embraced this approach and the impact has been significant.

Contrast the permissive parent with the authoritarian parent. The latter style is often too strict and dictatorial. It may suffocate the child into rebellion and very poor choices. It will likely harm the short and long-term relationship with the parents.

In the middle of the two is the authoritative parent who maintains reasonable guidelines and consequences. This ought to be a favored approach of parents as its short and long-term benefits maintain the spiritual, physical, mental and emotional well-being of the child.

When I was visiting my father's house for a weekend, my friend and I decided to toilet paper someone's house. I met this friend, whom we will call Jerry, when I was in the 3rd grade while visiting my father on a weekend. Despite his terrible influence on me growing up, Jerry is one of the only loyal friends I have left from childhood.

On this particular weekend, Jerry and I were packing up a duffle bag with toilet paper at about two in the morning. My father had woken up from his sleep and walked to the kitchen to grab a drink of water. He walked right by us. We were caught red-handed. Not knowing what else to say, we asked him if he wanted to join us. My father's response? "Be in before the sun comes up."

Granted, all we had in mind that night was relatively harmless vandalism, but my father did not know that. For all he knew, the vandalism was just one of many things we had planned for the night, each worse than the next. This possibility did not appear to concern him in the slightest.

So you see, I had free reign at my father's house. However, this was not the case at my mother's house.

My mom's house sat on ¾ of an acre and our house sat back a few hundred feet from the road. This relative seclusion made it seem sometimes that we actually lived on a small farm. As anyone knows who lives on a farm of any size, there are chores to be done every day. One day, I had a friend from school over with me and I forgot to do my chores. My step-dad approached and asked if I finished my daily responsibilities. I confessed that I had not. This prompted my step-dad to say, "Go get the paddle."

Understand this: Fear the paddle.

It was at least eighteen inches long and a half inch thick. It had three or four air holes in it to give it smooth sailing into your bottom end. I knew what was coming and why it was coming. I bent over and my step-dad properly placed the paddle in the most uncomfortable spot on the backside, near the bottom where the butt meets the hamstring; too high and you hit the lower back. A blow to the center hits directly into fattest part of the butt... and honestly doesn't hurt very much. My step-dad delivered the paddling with expert precision.

On this day, along with the perfectly placed swats, there was also public humiliation. My friend saw the whole thing.

Paddling a child today may have you in court facing child abuse allegations. Despite what some psychologist argue, spanking your child will not destroy them. However, I'm not necessarily making a case for paddling. What I'm saying is that children need consequences for their bad behaviors. Unfortunately, even if we do not ignore disobedience altogether, we virtually applaud it. "Let children be children," they say.

Even the less severe options for punishing disobedience in days gone by have been defanged. For example, when I was growing up, if I was sent to my room there wasn't anything to do but mope. It was not a fun experience. Today, *if* children are sent to their rooms, they have access to a TV, computer, tablet, cell phone, iPod, and a plethora of other options to remain entertained.

This refusal to correct bad behaviors and attitudes, my friends, is one reason why we are where we are today. Too many parents are refusing or afraid to parent. If parents won't administer appropriate and effective 'checks' on dangerous attitudes and behaviors, why should we be surprised when kids follow through on them when they get older?

I get strange looks from my students and athletes when I give them expectations and consequences for not fulfilling those expectations. It is amazing how many excuses they give for not meeting them, and how absurd the excuses often are. It's never their fault, you see, but someone else's.

I could not get away with that when I was child when I was with my mother. I took the responsibilities for my failures and received even more consequences if I tried to make excuses or lie.

Between those two choices, which does common sense tell you is more likely in real life to lead to disappointing failures and self-destructive behaviors which in turn generate even more disappointment?

My step-dad provided me with perhaps the most stable discipline growing up. I learned: "Do what you are supposed to do, do it right, or take your consequences." This is a great lesson to learn. Coupled with his example of a strong work ethic, my step-dad's influence of discipline was very positive.

Yet, at the same time, there was no direct or intentional godly leadership other than work hard and take responsibility for your actions. Let me give you an example of a missed opportunity to intentionally lead his step-children.

My brother and I were cleaning out a little closet tucked away upstairs in our house. We came across a red case that opened like a brief case. Inside? One condom and a small booklet on sex. This would have been a great opportunity for him to address the birds and the bees. The case was closed and we moved on.

The truth is, I cannot recall at any time where anyone sat down and talked to me about sex. I have no recollection of any *biblical* conversations about sex, drugs, or alcohol—and I went to a Christian grade school and a Christian high school. Neither my mother, father, nor step-dad ever sat down and talked about the physical, mental, or spiritual consequences of sex.

My father worked hard to pay child support and then, after my grandfather had his stroke, my father helped take care of him. Almost *forty* years after first becoming unexpectedly pregnant with my brother at the age of sixteen, my mother earned her college degree! Forty years! How is that for work ethic and persistence? Sure, my step-dad missed an opportunity to talk about the 'birds and the bees,' but his firm discipline and his own work ethic helped put me on the 'straight and narrow.' So, I don't want anyone thinking that I believe that not getting around to having an intentional conversation about sex does not necessarily make you a poor parent.

Like many others, I suspect that my parents expected the godly leadership to come from the parochial school we were sent to. Who could blame them, right? Isn't that how Christian schools are 'sold'? Is providing biblical leadership difficult (at the very least, you have to actually read the Bible and contemplate how to apply it!) and sometimes uncomfortable? No problem, just send them to the Christian school. The Christian school system will provide the parenting! Leave the godly leadership to the professionals!

While our elementary school had weekly worship, religion lessons and confirmation classes, I was never part of a serious conversation about drugs, sex, or alcohol. I don't recall any real conversations about being godly men or women. After elementary school, I went to a Christian high school, and I had the same experience there, too.

Just as my parents were not necessarily bad parents just because there was a lapse when it came to sex, drugs, and alcohol, my Christian schooling was not necessarily bad because it didn't tackle those topics well.

Looking back, my male theology teachers were the most prominent godly examples I knew, with Mr. Aumann being the one who stands out the most. Maybe that is because he was so tall! In his class, I remember having to read Frank Perretti's *This Present Darkness.* Regrettably, it was the only book I read in high school. His class was also the first time I had ever heard Christian music. An example that sticks out is "Shine" by the Newsboys, which received a Dove award in 1995.

For example, we took an Old Testament and New Testament class. In Old Testament, I was taught a quote from my teacher that has stayed with me to this day: "I am a unique child of God, full of potential." I have since adopted and adapted it for my classroom. That is probably one of the most direct attempts at spiritual influence other than content I can remember my first few years of high school.

Being a teacher now and working with some of the same individuals that once taught me, I know I was surrounded by godly men when I was a student.

Admittedly, I did not always pay attention, but I stand confident in my assessment. To my recollection, and I have not found anyone who can tell me otherwise, there weren't any serious conversations about sex, drugs, alcohol, and being a godly man or woman while attending my Christian high school.

Never once did any teacher pull me aside and ask about life—or smack me around and ask me, "What are you doing?"

We never had conversations or content which was directed toward us personally as young men or women.

We were not challenged to live godly lives; we weren't even told what that would look like.

Since most of my regrets later in life (and frankly, I regretted much of it the minute it happened) would revolve around bad decisions regarding 'sex, drugs, and alcohol,' it is tragic that I received so little guidance about these issues. I experimented with dangerous behaviors, for all the wrong reasons and without very many warnings about how those behaviors might negatively impact my life—or my soul.

As bad as all that is, a lot of the things I did involved other people. Sure, they were as rudderless as I was and fully complicit throughout, but I am sure that in many of those instances, they regret their actions, too. Instead of being a positive influence in their lives, I participated in and facilitated things they would wish they had never done.

In other words, the price for not being raised to be a godly young man was not just paid by me. Others would pay for it, too.

One could and perhaps should, point the finger at me. "How come you didn't go out of your way to grow and develop yourself?" is a fair question. I am guilty. I did not. I was more interested in chasing girls and winning games than I was in growing in godliness.

Yet, even if I had wanted to grow as a godly man, I would not have known where to start. There was no intentional guidance or resources provided, that I can remember, that proved to be instrumental in my development as a godly man.

Was I influenced? Undoubtedly. Positively? Yes, of course. Negatively? No doubt. Is it my fault? Yes. Could I have received more intentional direction on what being a young Christian man looked like? Absolutely, yes.[2]

A student once told me that my life story and experiences placed me in a better position to relate to all of the students. While I am thankful I am able to do so, I would take back all of those hurts and experiences in a heartbeat. I would do it all differently. I would maintain focus in high school. I would have placed less emphasis on being cool and wanted and more attention on what the teachers were talking about. I missed my opportunity. Will you miss yours?

Which way are you headed?
Towards or away from the cross of Christ?

---

[2] Dennis Prechel was the only staff member while in high school that I can remember paying much attention to my mental, emotional, physical and spiritual well-being. I had two class periods of "media assistant" with him in which he helped me with homework, asked about soccer and seemed interested in my life. I wasn't a superior athlete nor overly as academically intelligent or dramatic as other students who garnered teacher attention. To this day, he still reaches out and inquires as to my well-being.

Chapter 2

I Am Who I Am!

So where do we go from here? To figure out where we want to go, we have to find out where we are. We have to ask ourselves whether where we are is where we want to be, or are we meant to be somewhere else? Someone else?

At the time of this writing I will have been around the school's men's soccer program for almost twenty years. Like many conference games in high school athletics, ours were (are) usually intense, especially against certain opponents. More than once I have heard *Christian* athletes respond to negative outcomes with words more than unbecoming of what a young, godly man ought to say. Sometimes, across an entire width of an athletic field! When called out on their lack of self-control, which is usually directed at their own teammates or family members, the athletes often respond with the words, "It is what it is. I am who I am."

While emotions can run high and games can become intense, that is no excuse for that type of behavior. The truth is, who we are at times is disappointing and ugly. Who we are is not who we are supposed to be. Thankfully, a few of those players would now agree that it's a cop out to use that level of reasoning to justify our actions. It's an excuse to ignore consequences of the actions. More so, it is an excuse to be blind to the reality of who you are.

Years later as head coach of the same program, I challenged my players to look into the mirror after a deflating 1-2 loss. The problem with looking into the mirror is that we often do not like who we see. Worse yet, when we look to see who we are and see that it is terribly flawed, we often remain apathetic. To become something else seems impossible, so we justify to ourselves and others actions and behaviors that we know to be disgusting. We rationalize away the implications with comments like, "It is what it is" and, "No one is perfect."

Unfortunately, the mere use of the word 'perfect' implies a standard. To say we aren't 'perfect' is to admit that we aren't meeting that standard. The rationalization wants to have its cake and eat it too, acknowledging with one side of the mouth that we fail to live up to a standard but insisting with the other side of the mouth that one should be judged as if there is no standard at all and one simply can't help being what they are.

The rationalization falls apart when applied to other scenarios.

How does this sound to you: "The girl was completely embarrassed and humiliated by my disrespect for her. But who cares? This is who I am. She'll have to get over it."

More examples? What about this one: "I was so high, I have no idea how I got home. I mean, I know I put people's lives in danger, but this is who I am. I am who I am."

Or, "We were so drunk that neither one of us knew what we were doing. I did what?! Oh, who cares, it is what it is."

Or, "I got angry and punched that guy in the face. But this is who I am and it is what it is."

Why not go further?

"Your Honor, I admit I raped the girl, but I am who I am."

"Your Honor, I admit I ran over the person while I was driving drunk, but since I have no recollection of my own and had no control of myself at the time, I should not be held accountable for what happened."

"Your Honor, yes, I flew into a rage and bashed in that guy's skull with a baseball bat. But, I've always had a temper. I was born this way."

Thankfully, very few people extend their rationalizations to their logical conclusions, but that does not make the rationalization any less irrational.

The Skitguys have a video called "God's Original Masterpiece." It's worth watching if you have never seen it. In it is a catalog of significant thoughts that takes days to process. One line stands out to me. Summarized: "God loves you too much to leave you where you are at."

If we change it into a question it could look like this, "How much do you have to hate yourself to leave yourself where you are at?"

In other words, if you wanted to be proud (in a good way) of the person you are, wouldn't you want to take steps to improve? You must really hate yourself if you decide to just live with your failings and pretend they are just 'you' rather than working to see if 'just you' could become someone else.

It is in fact true that we are not 'perfect.' It is even true that there is nothing we can do to become perfect. Thanks be to God, that's the whole problem that Jesus came to resolve for us! At the same time, God has given us his Spirit. Do you think that the same God who was able to pay for the sins of all mankind, past, present and future, is unable to enter into you and not make a positive impact?

I believe that with wise parenting and godly correction, young people can be brought to see that there is hope.

Consider the lessons that children learn when they are not firmly shown that their conduct is wrong. Note: no one says this to them; they infer and absorb it as the logical implication of their upbringing. When they are not corrected, they assume there is nothing worth correcting. If it was wrong, someone would have told them! And why is it not worth correcting? Well, maybe it is because they couldn't help it, anyway.

Now consider the lessons learned by inference if a child receives discipline. First, of course, they learn that there are indeed attitudes and behaviors that are wrong. Secondly, they perceive that they couldn't possibly be disciplined for something if it was not believed that the child could have done otherwise. Thirdly, as they grow up and do in fact bring at least some of their behaviors under control, they learn (obviously), that they do have some control over their behaviors.

For those raised with appropriate discipline, a day comes when they realize that no matter how hard they try, they still say or do things they regret. They still do things they are ashamed of. If the child has been raised on biblical principles, the child will now learn firsthand about grace and mercy—first as to how it applies to themselves, thanks to God and Jesus' sacrifice, and secondly how to extend grace and mercy to others.

What young people fail to see is how their actions influence their future.

At the high school where I teach, seniors are granted a built in "skip day." They sleep in, but I still wake up and enjoy the opportunity of going into school. Without seniors to teach, I mosey my way into the freshmen theology class. I have a lovely chat with them about where they want to go and what regrets they may have at the end of their four years of high school.

After we discuss that, I 'up' the game. I ask them about any possible regrets they may have at the end of college. Their 40's? Their 50's? One of the last questions I ask is regarding regrets one might have on their death bed.

Heavy.

How many young people have been asked to look ahead sixty

years and imagine what kinds of things they might regret? Unfortunately, the reality is that the things they might regret six decades hence are related to the decisions they will be making *right now*. Or, at least, very soon.

Doesn't it then make sense to prepare them for these decisions?

Many parents hesitate to discipline their children because they think it is 'unloving' to call attention to their child's faults. I would challenge those parents themselves to think ahead sixty years or so, and ask themselves how 'unloving' it was to the child to let them stumble from one shameful act to another, accumulating regret upon regret.

If you love your child, you will do what you can, while you have the opportunity, to ensure (to the best of one's ability, anyway) that when your child reaches old age, your child will not be ashamed of the life he or she lived.

Well, just how does one ensure that?

Beyond providing godly discipline, which I have now repeatedly stressed, it is imperative that one talks about these 'heavy' topics early and often, striving to bring to bear biblical principles and show how they can assist them. But this book is written for young people who will be parents in the future, who might already be saddled with baggage from their upbringing. What can they do?

Back to the freshmen.

I continue to ask them questions and they almost always know the answer without me having to spell it out.

"If your parents are more inclined to be partiers, will you be more inclined to be a partier, as well?"

"If you are more inclined to be a partier, what type of people do you suppose you would be inclined to associate with?"

The answer to question two is obvious. It's hard to have a party if you are by yourself. You party with other people who also want to party. You can see how these questions pretty much answer themselves.

Question three is along the same lines:

> If you are more inclined to be a partier, and associate with partiers, will your college experience will reflect that?

Well, yea, obviously. If you party in high school, then it is likely you will continue the pattern into college and beyond.

It is not set in stone, of course, but experience tells us that one thing begets a similar thing.

If you plant a tomato seed, the result is going to be a tomato plant. That's so obvious, it seems absurd to think otherwise. And yet, we tend to think that if we are immersed in certain attitudes and behaviors while we are young, we'll magically 'grow out of them,' or, I should say, 'grow into' something else entirely.

Pressing the point with the freshmen, I now ask a fourth question.

If you spend your time at parties and drinking, is there a good chance your future spouse will be the kind of person who likes to party and drink? The odds seem strong.

We move the conversation from whom we get married to, to how you will raise your children. For me, my parents partied and lived more of a secular lifestyle in keeping with the spirit of the 1960s and 1970s. According to the logic I've been spelling out, it should be no surprise that my own lifestyle as a young man was fairly secular. The point I'm trying to make with the freshmen is that they shouldn't just be thinking about themselves when we discuss these issues. They should understand that how they proceed will almost certainly have a direct impact on the health and well-being of their own children.

The logical progression of the whole talk culminates into this critical question: "Who is it that you have been called to be?"

The decisions made as young men and women shape whom they become later. This is common sense. Perhaps up to this point, the young freshmen have been at the mercy of their circumstances. They can't help how they were raised. But now, they have the ability to make their own decisions. They might not be able to change where they are at that moment, or how they arrived in that place, but they are able to change where they are going and what kind of person they will be when they will get there.

One of the main lessons I try to instill with them (and in my classes, generally) is that who we choose to associate with is a very important factor. We cannot help but be influenced by the people we spend time with. If we spend a lot of time around dishonorable people, that will 'rub off' on us. (Lie down with dogs, wake up with fleas!) Likewise, if you spend time around honorable people, that will 'rub off' on you, as well. Now, up to that point, whomever they spend their time with was largely dictated by their own parents.

However, now they get to choose who they will surround themselves with. They should choose wisely.

Maurice Clarett, a football player, had a bright future ahead of him. Unfortunately, he had made some decisions that caught up with him including a high speed chase that resulted in his arrest and the officers finding guns and alcohol in his car. When reflecting on his past, Clarett said, "Show me your friends and I will show you your future."

For those with ears to hear and eyes reading with purpose to grow, those are powerful words.

Take a quick look at your friends and the influence they have on you. If you are of the stubborn type and come to the conclusion that your friends do not influence you because you are independent, you are kidding yourself. If you think you are not being influenced by your friends or influencing them, you are being naïve.

For me, the self-destructive behaviors I was playing with in high school were blunted by opportunities and other influences. My first year at college, I roomed with my older brother. Thankfully, he was not in the 'party' scene and was making a serious attempt to live a godly life. My girlfriend, too, was endeavoring to abide by biblical principles. I did not realize at the time how critical these influences were at the time in changing the trajectory of my life.

Hopefully, my readers will be more pro-active than I was. Choose your friends wisely!

Never mind who you want to be: Cool. Accepted. Sexy. Popular. Who are you pretending to be? Who were you pretending to be before you slipped into *who you are*?

Of course, this assumes that who you are and what you do is negative. You may very well be a mature young man or woman. You could have your head on straight. Be academically focused. If you already treat people with respect, perhaps the examples I have given are lost on you. Props to you. Keep it up! And remember Galatians 6:1 and 2 John 1:8.

But if you can already see that you are falling into bad habits, it's not too late. God loves you too much to leave you the way you are!

If you are not who you are supposed to be,
then who are you meant to be?

Chapter 3

Being Intentional

It wasn't until the sixth or seventh year of teaching that I actually became intentional about who I was and where I was going. My relationship with my wife was strained as I had invested emotionally in everyone and everything but her. I had effectively deserted the relationship. The word 'divorce' was in the air.

I was too busy admiring myself in the mirror to look more carefully at what it revealed. It wasn't until the mirror was broken over my head that I became aware of who I was and where I was going in life. Others could see what was happening, and finally five or six people decided to challenge me on it. That meeting brought the issues (me) out into the open. I had no choice but to face the unhealthy marriage. Having my marriage called out, called me out as a man and forced me to wrestle with how my own life was inconsistent with what I taught in class.

Since that time I have taken many steps on my own volition to grow and take ownership of the faith and life entrusted to me by God. God has continued to grow me into the unique child of God He desires. The last twenty-five or more years have provided me with excellent learning opportunities, at my own expense, that I am able to share with the students. I have literally been there, done that.

One topic of conversation in "Applied Christianity," the name of the class for 12th grade theology, is marriage and relationships. This is one of the most intriguing and enjoyable topics of the school year. We talk about everything from Mountain Dew cans, backrubs, dating, and the biblical principal of "one flesh" unions. An important part of the conversation revolves around what a godly man and woman looks like in the world today.

The biblical view is much different than the worldly point of view, and that is why it offers so many different opportunities for conversations. Many students form their attitudes and behaviors from a secular point of view as opposed to one which stems from an understanding of the Word of God. A quote often used in class sounds like this: "Too many individuals read the world into the Word instead of reading the Word into the world." We often prioritize our earthly citizenship above our heavenly citizenship. Often our values and morals align more with the world as opposed to the Word, when in reality, the Word should be the great influencer.

Two-thousand eighteen marked my eighteenth year of having the opportunity to educate and mentor young men and women. I have been married for almost twenty years. I am not claiming to have all of the answers. Nonetheless, I will propose that coaching, teaching and being married for two decades has allowed me to see how obvious it is that the youth need a more direct and *intentional* conversation about relationships and being godly men and women. There are so many young men who are in relationships, coming out of relationships, or have never been in a relationship before (that covers everyone, doesn't it?) that have no clue that how they proceed in these relationships matters for the present and into the future. (Obviously, there are some that do, but not nearly enough to be a comfort.)

1 Timothy 3 provides us with an excellent starting point for a conversation on what a godly man looks like living in a secular, non-religious world.

The movie *Beware of Christians,* when discussing marriage and relationships, quips that when you are in junior high you go to your junior high friends for dating relationships. When you are in high school you go to your high school friends. This is probably true, but is it prudent?

When was the last time a young man went out of his way to ask an older man for godly wisdom on relationships or being a godly man? Would that advice be the same advice offered by one's high school friends? If I were in high school asking my friends for dating advice, the encouragement would undoubtedly and ashamedly had been, "get some." (And I went to a Christian school.)

An older, wiser person would hopefully lead them into a further discussion on sexual purity and godly leadership, and hopefully a discussion based on 1 Timothy 3. This chapter of 1 Timothy will be the basis for the rest of the book.

The apostle Paul is writing a letter to a young man named Timothy. In his third chapter to Timothy, Paul writes, "Whoever aspires to be an overseer desires a noble task." Thus, the context of the conversation from Paul to Timothy concerns the conduct of an "overseer." Given that, someone might be tempted to dismiss 1 Timothy 3 as not relating to them personally, because they are not going to be a pastor of a church.

While it is true that the context is relating to a leader of a congregation, it is clear that a big part of the qualifications for being an 'overseer' is simply that he must be a godly man. Moreover, it is implied that a godly man will be a leader of his family; hence, if a man is not already leading in his family, the question is how he could possibly be a leader of the church.

If we have wanted to know what a godly man 'looked' like, we can thank Paul for painting us a picture:

> Now the overseer is to be above reproach, faithful to his wife, temperate, self-controlled, respectable, hospitable, able to teach, not given to drunkenness, not violent but gentle, not quarrelsome, not a lover of money. He must manage his own family well and see that his children obey him, and he must do so in a manner worthy of full respect. (If anyone does not know how to manage his own family, how can he take care of God's church?) He must not be a recent convert, or he may become conceited and fall under the same judgment as the devil. He must also have a good reputation with outsiders, so that he will not fall into disgrace and into the devil's trap.

We may grant that godliness doesn't necessarily mean "able to teach," but surely we don't think that *only* the pastor is to be "above reproach, faithful to his wife, temperate," and so on! Are we going to say that the pastor must have a "good reputation with outsiders" but the rest of us shouldn't be concerned with such things? Are we going to say that only the pastor should be "not given to drunkenness" but the rest of us can spend our time getting drunk out of our minds? Nonsense.

Beyond this, but also extending the logic, we see hints that it is not *only* the "overseer" who must exhibit leadership. Unless we believe that only the pastor should "manage his own family well," we can see that, at minimum, one expectation of godly manhood is that he be the *leader* of his own family.

And what would that look like?

> ... above reproach, faithful to his wife, temperate, self-controlled, respectable, hospitable, ... not given to drunkenness, not violent but gentle, not quarrelsome, not a lover of money.

Hopefully no one seriously believes that Paul's mentioning of these principles relates only to pastors. However, before anyone gets any crazy ideas that they will only apply to men, consider that Paul continues and says, "*In the same way*, the women are to be worthy of respect, not malicious talkers but temperate and trustworthy in everything." [Emphasis mine.]

Hopefully no one is so desperate to justify themselves that they will assert a further absurdity, that only married people are to live godly lives. There are plenty of passages (such as Ephesians 5:1) that refute that nonsense.

But where I'm really going with this is that all of us are called to be godly examples.[3] This means that whether you like it or not, you are a leader whenever you interact with other Christians and non-Christians. That is, you are a leader, in your own way, all the time. You may not have the title of a 'pastor,' or a 'youth director,' but be sure you are leading others by your words, actions, lack of words, and lack of actions.

You may be uncomfortable with this designation as a leader, but get used to it. *Everyone is a leader.* That does not mean everyone's leadership is good. People can lead others positively or negatively.

Some people have titles as leaders because they have earned degrees or have been placed in certain 'leadership' roles. Strictly speaking, their responsibilities are different than yours. This does not disqualify you from being a leader, as everyone leads. Leadership guru John Maxwell writes in *The 21 Irrefutable Laws of Leadership* that "leadership is influence."

Be sure, you are influencing others, intentionally or unintentionally. Your family, friends, acquaintances, and strangers are constantly assessing you. If you are prone to coarse, rude or lewd language (Ephesians 5), then a friend of yours who may have been hesitant to talk that way before may be more likely to do it themselves.

Let me give you an example from my own life:

In the 5th or 6th grade, I was riding my bike around the neighborhood and met a kid who lived a couple streets over. He had no trouble swearing, dropping F-Bombs almost every sentence. Within a few days of meeting this new kid near my mother's house, I was swearing as much as my new friend. Of course, you know

---

[3] See also Matthew 5:16 and 2 Peter 2:12.

already that such behavior wasn't tolerated at home. I definitely would have been eating soap like poor Ralphie from the movie *A Christmas Story* if I had not checked myself. The point is, my new 'friend' had made it easier for me to engage in behaviors that I knew for a fact would be condemned by my parents at home. To put it even more starkly, this relationship made it easier for me to engage in conduct I knew to be wrong. This 'friend' was a leader.

Your friends are paying attention to what you do and how you do it. You have the choice to lead positively or negatively.

Now, you may even be thinking that you don't lead because you are just 'chill,' choosing to not aggressively lead one way or the other. You do not encourage your friends to be of honor, integrity, and respect, but you also do not encourage your friends to be liars, cheats, and disrespectful. Unfortunately for you, it doesn't matter. If they are lying and cheating and you do not say anything about it, you are influencing them. You have given them implicit permission to carry on and have influenced them to do so.

"Influencing" should be translated as, "leading."

One of my favorite leadership principles comes from the United States Marine Corps (USMC). It is simple and true, yet powerful: "Ductus Exemplo." It means, "Leadership by Example."

There are many books which discuss this leadership principle including a personal favorite, *The 9 Secrets of Marine Corps Leadership You Must Know to Win in Business.*

One does not have to read a book to know how powerful one's example is. The author of 1 John echoes this point in Chapter 3:16:

> This is how we know what love is: Jesus Christ laid down his life for us. And we ought to lay down our lives for our brothers and sisters.

While we do not want to reduce Jesus' significance to merely being an example of how to live, his example was nonetheless a powerful one.[4] Dying for someone is the highest service we can do for someone. Jesus definitely did not have to die for anyone, yet he did anyway. The impact of this decision literally changed the visible and invisible world forever. In this passage, we are explicitly called to do for others what Jesus did for us—even to the point of death.

Similarly, the value of our own lives far exceeds the simple fact

---

[4] And yet, see 1 Peter 2:21, Luke 6:40, and 1 Cor. 11:1.

that they are examples for others. Yet, that does not change the fact that you and I both cannot help but lead by example.

In *A Christmas Story*[5] there is a scene where Ralphie has his mouth washed out with soap for poor language. Ralphie's mother interrogates him and demands that he give up the source for such language. The whole neighborhood, including Ralphie, knows full well that the 'source' was his own father. He doesn't dare say that aloud, so he blames it on someone else, getting that kid into loads of trouble. Regardless of this misdirection, our point is made:

Our decisions—expressed verbally, non-verbally, in action or lack of action—not only have lasting consequences for ourselves, but influence other people.

Students and athletes frequently ask me why intentionally setting an example is important. While there are many passages we could look at it, 2 Corinthians 5:19-21 provides a most powerful answer:

> That God was reconciling the world to himself in Christ, not counting people's sins against them. And he has committed to us the message of reconciliation. We are therefore Christ's ambassadors, as though God were making his appeal through us. We implore you on Christ's behalf: Be reconciled to God. God made him who had no sin to be sin for us, so that in him we might become the righteousness of God.

What is Paul's answer to that question of, "Why worry about what example we set?" Because we are God's ambassadors. Christ has spoken to us the message of reconciliation in his own blood. God has given us this new creation through Christ and now he makes his appeal to others, through us, so that they too may know of the love of God.

If my life does not reflect this love, others will take note. Christ has loved us, am I therefore going to harass others? Be disrespectful to others? Mock others? That is definitely not the spokesperson we have been called to be. Being a good—and godly—example matters because God is expecting us to share his love with others. If that love is not being shared, then what are we doing with the life entrusted to us by God?

Throughout our lives, our roles will change. Today, you might

---

[5] If you have not seen this classic movie, you must watch it at least once!

only be a college student. Tomorrow, you might be a parent or a coach. Perhaps at some point you will be a teacher, or an administrator. What it means to be God's ambassador, and what that looks like, might vary in some respects depending on what vocation(s) we happen to be in at the moment. But let's turn again to 1 Timothy 3 for some important reminders and direction:

> Now the overseer is to be above reproach, *faithful to his wife*, temperate, self-controlled, respectable, hospitable, able to teach, not given to drunkenness, not violent but gentle, not quarrelsome, not a lover of money. He must manage his own *family* well and see that *his children* obey him, and he must do so in a manner worthy of full respect. (If anyone does not know how to manage *his own family*, how can he take care of God's church?) [Emphasis added.]

It is obvious from this passage that Paul sees our life within the family as being crucially important. It is also plain that Paul believes that how we conduct ourselves within our families will carry over into our everyday life. This is no doubt true, and what it means is that as parents we should take our example to our children very seriously. Not only do we make an indelible mark on our own children through our influence, but who we are within the household will manifest outside it.

I was never aware of the power of my influence or the influences surrounding me growing up. My parents influenced me both positively and negatively. I am who I am today largely as a result of their parenting and their choices. I have included some examples from my own life to demonstrate how we are influenced by our parents, friends, and society. And yet, there comes a point where we recognize that it is we, ourselves, who are doing the influencing. There comes a point where we cannot blame—or credit—our upbringing for where ever it is we stand now, and we make our own choices.

If you understand that your choices today will influence not only where you are tomorrow, but might in fact have impact for years, especially as it concerns how you will raise your very own children, you will begin to understand why I have emphasized why you must be intentional. Today influences tomorrow. If you know that and understand that, why wouldn't you intentionally aim to be a positive influence?

Understanding the powerful maxim that everyone leads is important. It means we cannot escape our responsibility that our lives set an example for others. There are no excuses. Later in 1 Timothy 4, Paul exhorts his young leader, “Don’t let anyone look down on you because you are young, but set an example for the believers in speech, in conduct, in love, in faith and in purity.” Living in such a way that you are a godly example is not something you put off until you are an adult. The Bible makes it plain that young or old, married or single, whatever your station, we are each called to follow Christ’s example which means also living as an example.

How and in which direction will you lead today?

Part II

Chapter 4

What Do They Say About You?

Now the overseer is to be **above reproach**, faithful to his wife, temperate, self-controlled, respectable, hospitable, able to teach, not given to drunkenness, not violent but gentle, not quarrelsome, not a lover of money.

Above Reproach

Greek Word αφνεπιωληπτος
Transliterated: Anepileptos

Pronounced: an-ep-eel'-ape-tos

If we have not already put enough pressure on ourselves being referred to as leaders and ambassadors of God, let's add more. One of the first qualifications given to Timothy by Paul is that a leader should be above reproach.

According to a variety of concordances, the Greek word "anepileptos" means, without rebuke or never caught doing anything wrong, blameless (Biblehub.com). Personally, I do not like this definition, not because it is wrong, but because it is probably accurate and it leaves me without excuses. As someone who is designated as a leader within a school, my conduct must be one in which I am never caught doing anything wrong. My words are to be spoken so that any student, parent, athlete, visitor, cannot rebuke me for me being in the wrong.

This weighs heavily on me because the class I teach is called "Applied Christianity." As one can imagine, the class is about what it looks like to apply the various aspects of Christianity to one's life. Anyone knows that it is very difficult to trust someone if their actions do not match up with their words. If I talk about love but only hate, no student in their right mind will listen to me, or even should. If I speak of love and respect, but walk onto the basketball court and intentionally and maliciously demean a player or another coach, any credibility is lost.

Here is an example of a former student speaking on the necessity to be above reproach. He was attending a Big 10 University. Like many of his friends, he had attended private school his entire life, but continued his education at a secular school. Without knowing too many details, the student recalled a conversation he had with someone who was a Muslim. Apparently the two of them had frequented the same parties, drinking the same alcohol, and at least one of them behaving in a way which violated their religious beliefs. The Muslim student asked the Christian what he was doing at the party drinking and getting intoxicated. Initially stunned by the question, he probed for an appropriate response while his friend retorted, "I thought you were a Christian."

Apparently, the Muslim correctly perceived there was a contradiction between the individual's profession of faith and actions. Clearly, at least in this moment, the person was not above reproach and definitely was caught doing something the other student thought was wrong. This isn't a statement of condemnation. We are simply pointing out that inconsistency between profession of faith and the actions of one's faith manifested are important. As a soccer and basketball coach at a Christian school, I must be very "wise in the way you act toward outsiders; make the most of every opportunity. Let your conversation be always full of grace, seasoned with salt, so that you may know how to answer everyone."[6]

Of course Paul is not talking about coaching athletics, but he is reminding us here and elsewhere in Scripture that opportunities abound—opportunities to be a positive ambassador of God—or a negative one. Consider this story:

In 2014, we were playing against a rival team for the district championship. In the closing minutes of the game, we were denied what was an obvious (to the assistant referee and everyone else it seemed) penalty kick that would have given us an easy opportunity

---

[6] Colossians 4:5-6.

to tie the game. I was furious that the opportunity was denied, but I could not lose my bearing. If I lost my bearing, so too would my players. After the game was a different story, and I wish this was not the case. I immediately went up to the referee to demand an answer as to why he chose to override his assistant's call. His answer was unsatisfactory to say the least. I disagreed and I let him know. I didn't swear. I didn't demean him or his value as a person. I did, however, let it be known that his decision and lack of integrity for the game was disappointing. The damage was done. I am supposed to be above reproach. Look at me and you are to find no fault or hypocrisy. Here I was giving an earful to the referee.

Some of you may very well agree that he should have been verbally undressed. However, I knew that I failed. Certainly that referee has a poor image of the Christian school I work for, now. He certainly could have concluded that if this is what a Christian school and a Christian man looks like, he'd want no part of it. Only a few people were close enough to hear or see anything, but I knew. I knew my behavior was not above reproach. If that referee sees me again, he will definitely remember me and I will not be without blame.

Shortly after my conversation with the referee one of my players said, "Thanks." For what? The player was thanking me for letting the referee have it. Sigh. Every game and every practice I try to conduct myself in a way that will be above reproach and blame and shame, only to have one incident undermine it. Unfortunately, so many athletes believe you should be yelling and screaming at the referees for bad calls. And for some, if you do not do that, you are not fighting for the team.

If I swear, lie, steal, openly and deliberately malign someone, anything I have done in the classroom, by action and deed is undermined. It's a heavy burden to carry and I definitely am not perfect. Yet, it is assumed that I am, and when I do make a mistake, any credibility I have is undermined. You may conclude that I am being a bit dramatic, but it is true.

I certainly cannot encourage my students to live a life worthy of the calling they have received, only to have them find me on a social media network doing keg-stands, or with my eyes red. Would you listen to me? I would not, nor would I expect you to. Consider what is at stake. If I am an ambassador of God, as if he were making his appeal to others through me, I would have failed miserably. We only have one opportunity to make a first impression. After we have built up an image of whom we are or are not in Christ, our actions either confirm or deny that image.

It's not fair, but it happens. Brennan Manning summarizes the significance of this in this way:

"The greatest single cause of atheism in the world today is Christians: who acknowledge Jesus with their lips, walk out the door, and deny him by their lifestyle. That is what an unbelieving world simply finds unbelievable."

The young man in the college story mentioned earlier speaks to the truth of this statement. People have certain expectations of Christians and they wait for the one moment they can dismiss it as illegitimate. Unfortunately, many of us make this dismissal very easy. It's not fair that people reject the veracity of Christianity on the basis of *our* actions, but they do. If you do a quick look on the Internet, you can find many examples of atheists pointing to the bad decisions of Christians as their reasons for dismissing the truth of Christianity.

As a young man, it is important to understand that you will not be perfect. We will fall short of God's holiness and we will be forgiven. The whole point of Christ's coming was to bring this forgiveness: who needs a doctor, if one is not sick?[7] In no way does this mean that we bathe in the desires of the flesh. Confronting this very notion, Paul says in Romans 6:1-2, "What shall we say, then? Shall we go on sinning so that grace may increase? By no means! We are those who have died to sin; how can we live it any longer?"

Strange as it is to say, as a young man, you may have it easier, but the reasons are not very flattering. Simply put, society's expectations for young men today are very low to begin with. It is expected that you behave and think a certain way. Mistakes or poor decisions are brushed aside as "kids being kids." Of course, there is some basis for giving "kids" more latitude. Younger people have less life experience than others and therefore make poorer decisions than older people.

However, it doesn't have to be this way. My firm belief that young people have the ability to make wise choices, sparing them from uncomfortable consequences and priming them for future health, happiness, and spiritual wholeness is one of the catalysts for this book in the first place.

Nonetheless, one only needs to listen to certain music or watch

---

[7] Matthew 9:11-13.

certain television shows to come to a conclusion that if you are not drinking at the bar or having sex, you are doing it wrong. If those are the expectations we have for our men of the world, we should not be surprised at the society we live in today. We will discuss the consequences of such a mentality when we discuss more examples below.

Perhaps you are not interested in setting an example as an ambassador for God and do not see the necessity or benefits of living a life above reproach. Consider these examples and their impact.

Up to this point and time, you have simply lived a life that is consistent with the cultural norm. "Kids will be kids" is your motto and your parents' motto. Within the past couple of years, you have dated a few girls, off and on. No big deal of course, you didn't have sex and certainly did not have any children out of wedlock. Crisis adverted. But, you did fool around with girls. In fact, you made a name for yourself as a 'player.' Kids will be kids, right?

Then one day you meet this girl who you really like. She's smart, funny, kind, and does well in school. After a while, you work up the courage to introduce yourself to her. Perhaps at a party, or an athletic event, or a ... well, where doesn't matter! The damage was done long ago. Your reputation is already out there. You, my friend, are not without blame. The word on the street is that you like the girls. You are more than happy to make out with them, maybe even date them for a while before moving on to the next. Your present situation has been influenced by your past behaviors. You approach the girl but you do so 'under reproach.' She has no time for you because she knows you disrespect women. Hiding behind 'kids will be kids' and thinking no one will notice, or that there might not still be significant fallout, has ruined what might have been one of the best things to ever happen in your life.

Let's say you manage to get past your foul reputation and the two of you actually do get together. Maybe you even get married. Does that change how everyone else remembers you? You have made a name for yourself within the community. Now, imagine you interview for a job and the person interviewing knows you. He knows you because you once dated his niece and heard the story about how you left her humiliated at a party because she would not make out with you. Do you think you will get this job?

How might this have gone the other way? Consider: you have had two or three girlfriends in your short life, all of them relatively mature relationships. While out on dates you have treated the girls with utmost respect. If the parents wanted her home by 10:30 she was home by 10:15, or, at latest, 10:29. There were no games, no excuses, no shameless or pointless make out sessions. You are the kind of young man that a man would want his daughter to marry.

I wish I had been that guy, but instead, I was the guy with the 'rep.' While I certainly respected people, I was the one considered a 'player.'

When we talk about being 'above reproach,' perceptions matter.

One of my most awkward and humiliating moments of my life was in college when my mother-in-law called me out on this in rebuke. It is uncomfortable for me to share it, but it serves as an excellent story to highlight of what being above reproach looks like and why it matters.

At the time, I was a freshman in college and had been dating her daughter for a couple months. I was at her place. Her daughter and I 'spooned' on the couch while watching television in the basement. There wasn't any making out or anything else, we were simply on the couch lying down next to each other. My wife's mother did the old 'check the laundry trick.' Within seconds she had a basket worth of clothes and had made her way back upstairs, calling her daughter upstairs. I was oblivious to what was going on.

If I was in trouble for lying on the couch with her daughter I was guilty, but was it really that big of a deal? Minutes went by before I was called upstairs. There in the living room we sat, my future mother-in-law, my girlfriend (now wife), and myself—nervous, but not sure why. On the table in front of us was a porcelain bowl.

My mother-in-law began to talk about my going into the pastoral ministry and the image one projects. Even the slightest "chip in the bowl" denigrated the purity and perfection of the bowl. If I was having pre-marital sex, I most definitely would not have been "above reproach." My parishioners would find out about my sexual impurity and I would not be able to faithfully and effectively carry out the ministry of the Word.

Now, we weren't having sex. In fact, I thought it was a stretch to see a couple laying down the couch together and draw the conclusion that they must also be sexually active. Still, perceptions matter. Doubt was raised. My reputation was being shaped.

I share this story with my students every year that we talk about marriage and dating. The looks on the faces of my students is the same as what I was feeling on the inside when I was having "the talk" with my future mother-in-law. The truth of the matter is, as awkward as the conversation was, the mom simply cared about me, and of course her daughter. She was trying to protect both of us. I understand that now.

The concept and idea represented in my conversation with my mother-in-law are ones I discuss in my own classroom. I will make sure my own children understand it, too.

Your previous actions and behaviors will shape your present experiences. Those in turn will shape your future attitudes and behaviors. If you are a 'player' in high school, you will probably be a 'player' in college and beyond. If you party and get drunk in high school, you will probably do so in college, too. Habits are very hard to break! Yet, it isn't just about your conduct. It is also about how your conduct will be perceived by outsiders and how this might harm your ability to be an effective ambassador for God. If you have 'chips in the bowl,' people will notice, and you shouldn't be surprised if folks don't want to bring you out on the best occasions.

It would be tempting to play the sin card: "we all sin." However, there is a difference between acknowledging that we fail to meet God's high expectations for us and justifying and rationalizing our behavior. In other words, you will hear people say, "we all sin" when what they are really saying is, "I really want to be continuing doing 'x,' even though I know it is wrong. So, I'm gonna."

There is a big difference between making excuses for our mistakes and taking responsibility for those mistakes. This, too, relates to how we are perceived. Those who rationalize their bad behavior develop a reputation for doing so, while those who own up to their mistakes and try, genuinely, to grow from them, are taken note of. Eventually, whether or not you have made a good name for yourself or a bad name for yourself will make a difference in some part of your life. At that time, you will deeply regret your past actions, or praise God that he gave you the strength to be the kind of person God wanted you to be.

I have focused on the idea of being 'above reproach' in the context of dating and careers, with more than a nod towards how that might relate to the witness that gives to others. Since dating and finding a job are two areas that a young person will be grappling with very soon (if they aren't grappling with them already!) these seemed like good places to emphasize. However, there are many aspects of the idea. For example, are you known to be honest? Timely? Lazy?

Are you the kind of man that someone looks at says, "Now *that's* a young man." Or are you constantly being rebuked by Scripture, your parents, authority figures, and your friends? You do have the ability to impact how people answer that question! Better yet, in the future when others see your children, what will they say about them? Don't care? You should, because you will have taught them by your leadership.

When someone looks at you, what do they see?
Better question: who do they see?

What I tell the young women:

Ladies, take a look at the young man you are dating or are considering dating. Is he the kind of young man that when you see him, he is above reproach? Or, is he the young man who is always in trouble? If that's the case, consider your future with this young man. Why do you think he won't bring that trouble into your relationship? Is that really the future you want? If he is not the kind of young man you want to take home to your parents, that is a bad sign. Choose wisely.

Chapter 5

She Belongs to the Lord

> Now the overseer is to be above reproach, **faithful to his wife**, temperate, self-controlled, respectable, hospitable, able to teach, not given to drunkenness, not violent but gentle, not quarrelsome, not a lover of money.

Faithful to his *one* wife

Greek word: μια
Transliterated: mia

Pronounced: mee-ah

The Genesis account of creation leaves no doubt what God's intention of marriage looks like.

> But for Adam no suitable helper was found. So the LORD God caused the man to fall into a deep sleep; and while he was sleeping, he took one of the man's ribs and then closed up the place with flesh. Then the LORD God made a woman from the rib he had taken out of the man, and he brought her to the man. The man said, "This is now bone of my bones and flesh of my flesh; she shall be called 'woman,' for she was taken out of man." That is why a man leaves his father and mother and is united to his wife, and they become one flesh (Genesis 2:20-24).

God has an original paradigm for marital relationships which is repeated and supported throughout all of Scripture in a variety of places. All of that which God created was "good," including man, who is said to be made in God's image (Genesis 1:27). Part of the goodness given to man is free will. Man, having free will, took that which was good, and corrupted it. That's why you see places in Scripture where there is polygamy, incest, adultery, divorce. It happened but it does not mean that it is godly.[8]

---

[8] Bible scholars make a distinction between 'descriptive' language and 'prescriptive' language. The Bible *describes* many things people did that

Paul says that a bishop should be "husband of but one wife." This ties in with his later insight, that if one cannot manage his own family, he cannot manage the church. Like my mother-in-law pointed out, even the perception of sexual immorality could undermine my ability to minister within a congregation. Hopefully we have established well enough that Paul's counsel does not apply only to those who want to be an 'overseer.' It is absurd to suppose that the bishops cannot be sexually immoral, but everyone else can just have at it.

Given God's stated plan for marriage, how much that plan is emphasized within the Scriptures, and the fact that my book is written with unmarried young men in mind, who will eventually want to marry, a conversation about sexuality and marriage is obviously in order.

Here is the bottom line: Christian leaders (all of us!) are to be sexually pure.

What does this mean for you? Loads. What does this mean for your relationships? Loads. And what does this mean for your children? Loads. "But what does this have to do with children?" you say.

Ok, well, we are talking about sexuality, right? Does everyone understand where babies come from? It ought to go without saying that there will be a connection between our sexual conduct and our children. However, I have in mind even more than that. Remember that as leaders, we set a pattern for others to follow. As a parent, your attitude about sexuality will transfer over to your children, whether you like it or not. What follows, then, will be most immediately relevant to young people who are presumably a long way off from

---

God disapproved of and sometimes the Bible points out how God felt about the conduct and other times it doesn't. Just because the Bible *described* conduct, does not mean that the Bible *prescribes* that conduct. Most of the criticism of what the Bible contains does not take into account that God *himself* was opposed to what transpired. Readers need to bring their brain with them when reading the Bible. The fact that the Bible contains material that is embarrassing to God, and embarrassing to his people, actually lends it credibility; writers modern and ancient tend to whitewash their own history. Is the marital formula described in Genesis *prescriptive* or *descriptive?* Given that this formula is repeated several times in the Scriptures, including by Jesus himself, it is pretty clear that this formula is, in fact, prescriptive.

having children of their own, but that doesn't mean we should ignore this aspect of the issue. Besides, because of the very nature of the thing I'm talking about, it may be the case that having children may not be that far off at all.

Take a look at the music we listen to, the movies we watch, and the television we soak in daily. Consider the websites available to us 24/7, along with their many advertisements. It should be of no shock to anyone that sex is used to sell products. Commercials from web domains to candy use sexual innuendos to promote their product.

Young men are full of active hormones and companies know this and use it to their advantage. It is expected that you either have a girlfriend, a friend with benefits, or that you are just making out with whomever. Again, take a look at any of the supposed "popular movies" directed towards the youth today and sex and romance is at the core. If you are not making out with girls or seeking a relationship, then the implication is that there is something wrong with you.

I was not immune to that line of reasoning. For reasons I am not clear about, it was ingrained within me to always have a girlfriend or to look for one. I was never content with being single and before I found my wife, I was always chasing a girl.

People will claim that this is typical and there isn't anything to worry about, but I disagree. Remember, I work as a teacher and spend my entire working life around young adults. I have been there, done that, and seen it every day in the media and on the school campus. People are being hurt mentally, emotionally, physically, and spiritually. False expectations for relationships are being created without the youth being aware, and these expectations are causing harm.

Clearly these expectations are being absorbed from our sex-saturated media, but let's talk about pornography, which is a serious problem facing our society today. Please see the appendix, which includes links and references to some of the studies that show the harm that pornography is capable of inflicting.

I have provided a paragraph that summarized some of the most recent studies on pornography. Each underlined portion represents a link to the conclusions they are referencing which can be referenced using the appendix in the back of the book.[9]

Young men are especially prone to pornography.

Access to pornography is more accessible than it was when I was growing up. The Internet today obviously provides many opportunities for a young man. Never mind the existence of hardcore pornography, soft core pornography exists in various mediums and is prevalent on almost every television station in many programs. Even when it is not "sexual activity" between man and woman, there are still plenty of programs that show half-naked women dancing provocatively or behaving sexually.

The consequences go well beyond the effects on the young men who are more susceptible to our sex-saturated society. The effects on the men have effects on the women in multiple ways. For example, whether it is blatant pornography or more subtle imagery on television and other mediums, men have been led to conclude that women are supposed to look a certain way. I address this in class with many videos reminding men and women that the stereotypical "hot woman" does not exist. It is one of our more popular topics.

Pro tip: if a lustful thought tries to enter my mind I replace it with: "That's not my wife. Think about your wife." You can fight temptation by intentionally taking control of the things you think about.

What's a young man to do? If you ask your average evolutionist, a young person should be able to act on his hormones without any guilt or repression from their parents or religious institutions. Unfortunately, there is so much wrong with that ideology that is ignored. I hope you look at the studies I have referenced in the appendix! It is simply not true that acting out on one's sexuality, willy-nilly, will have no negative

[9] There are a growing list of studies that *do* find associations between solo porn use and arousal, attraction, and sexual performance problems. The underlined text refers to links you can find in the index. Findings include difficulty orgasming, diminished libido or erectile function (1, 2, 3, 4, 5, 6),negative effects on partnered sex, decreased enjoyment of sexual intimacy (1, 2, 3), less sexual and relationship satisfaction (1, 2, 3, 4), a preference for using Internet pornography to achieve and maintain arousal over having sex with a partner, and greater brain activation in response to pornography in those reporting less desire for sex with partners. Online porn use even correlates with abnormally low sexual desire in high school seniors.

consequences!

Try telling that to the young men watching pornography or viewing women in other mediums.

Every year in my classroom I give a survey to my students asking them why they believe women wear make-up. I ask both the young men and the women. The answers are astounding but revealing.

The typical answers (from both genders) are, so that they "look prettier," or, "because I do not like myself." The extreme answers, given politely, of course, include "without make-up, girls are ugly,' and from one young lady, "I don't like my face without it." I find these answers disheartening and discouraging.

We live in a world where there is a significant emphasis on external appearance. So much so, that the entire world is captivated by certain types of women and appalled by others. Where do you fit into this? I assume it is obvious to you that women are more than objects, despite how the media portrays them. How does the Bible think we should relate to women? One of the most challenging verses in the Scriptures, for me, is Ephesians 5:

> *Husbands, love your wives, just as Christ loved the church and gave himself up for her to make her holy,* cleansing her by the washing with water through the word, and to present her to himself as a radiant church, without stain or wrinkle or any other blemish, but holy and blameless. In this same way, husbands ought to love their wives as their own bodies. He who loves his wife loves himself. After all, no one ever hated their own body, but they feed and care for their body, just as Christ does the church— for we are members of his body. "For this reason a man will leave his father and mother and be united to his wife, and the two will become one flesh."[10]

From this passage, it is clear that God's interest in the relationship between a man and a woman goes well beyond that relationship. He actually uses marriage as a way to understand what Jesus did for us. But it is even more than that. Husbands are called to love their wives

---

[10] This is one of the aforementioned passages on the Genesis 'formula' for marriage that strongly argues for this 'formula' being prescriptive rather than descriptive.

in just the same way that Jesus loved the church. In case anyone has forgotten what Jesus did for the church, let me remind you: *he died for her.*

That is a very high bar being set for men! It certainly represents an entirely different set of expectations about women, too. Women are more than sexual objects to fulfill the husband's sexual desires. The wife is represented as having value in her own right, worthy of a man's most selfless efforts on her behalf. This is a far cry from the way that the world regards women, of course, but more than that, it signals that God's plan for marriage is nothing like the world's understanding of marriage. In God's plan, the happy, healthy, stable marriage between a man and a woman is a living image of Jesus' sacrifice for the church.

Wow.

Take a minute and think about that, considering this portrayal of relations between a man and a woman with just about anything you'll find on a screen.

Coming to grips with God's plan for marriage was a long, hard journey for me. I was exposed to porn early, thanks to the easy access of pornographic magazines at my father's house. False expectations of sexuality and relationships were created. I was not going around having sex, but my brain was being shaped. The thought patterns were being developed. Even when I was dating my eventual wife, I was very selfish. I was nowhere near ready to die for anyone, let alone her. It takes a long time to overcome the habits we absorbed over the course of years, and it has not been easy for me. However, with intentional and deliberate obedience to the Scriptures (see Romans 12:1-2) the thought patterns can be re-written. It becomes easier—and it is well worth it. Experiencing God's plan for marriage firsthand, I can tell you it is far more rewarding than acting out on the world's idea for it.

I've now said a lot about something you probably already knew: sex is everywhere. What you may not have taken the time to consider are the consequences of how you react to that reality. Perhaps now is that time. Let's think about how your attitudes may have been shaped to this point.

If your father treats your mother with great respect, there is a very good chance you will too. If he speaks words of affirmation often in front of you, he will model a behavior that will influence you.

However, do you perceive that women are nothing more than

sexual objects to be used at your disposal? Where did you get that idea? Does your father verbally abuse your mother? Does your father make snide comments about your mother's weight or appearance? Are there pictures of half-naked women on the walls in your garage? Does this sound anything like God's intention for relations between a man and a woman? Do you think Jesus has a poster of the naked church posted on the wall of his throne room? I don't think so.

Example is a powerful lesson. For better or for worse, what you have been exposed to as you grew up will have left a mark on your own attitudes. Understanding how this played out in your own life, don't you see that how you treat women and view sex will influence how your son views women and sex?

If you have experienced regrets and disappointments in these matters, don't you want to spare your own children from enduring the same pain? I know I do. If the legacy that has been left to you to this point from your own parents has been positive, don't take it for granted. While it may be more natural for you to set a healthy example for your children, it is critical that you are very intentional about being that example, and pondering just what kind of example you are being, and whether or not that is the kind of example you are setting.

Why? Due to our extremely sexualized society, you can expect that your children are going to be slammed from all sides with entirely different examples. Unless you rise to the challenge, even if you feel that you are being a positive example, your example might be overwhelmed by the hourly temptations presented in our media-drenched society.

Your son will be sexually curious. He will see images on television despite your best efforts. Recently my family and I were watching kids programming in the early evening and a commercial for an adult product appeared on the screen. What? We could not change the channel fast enough. But imagine if that is the usual type of content your child sees (or you). Will they (you) receive their sex education from the pornography you leave out or hang in your man cave? I hope not.

As you can imagine, I will be doing whatever I can to make sure my son views women and treats women appropriately. There will be no pornography in my house. No pinups on my walls! Certainly, while not manifested perfectly, I will show my son how much you are supposed to love a woman, and I will be using Christ as my guide as to how to do that.

I not only owe it to my wife to treat her as such, but I owe it to my son to show him the way. I owe it to his future girlfriends and wife. The last thing I want is for them is to be treated like objects because I failed as his father. I have a fight to fight. The media, his friends, and his hormones will all be fighting against my lesson. The best way to teach him such important lessons is to lead by example.

Habits and patterns regarding sexuality start young. Even things that we might consider to be innocent might in fact 'chip' away at our purity, or leave a blemish on the purity of another.

Consider this scenario. Let's say you and a girl in high school have been dating a few months, and by 'dating' we just means holding hands and passing notes. Well, as can be expected, things begin to progress. Finding yourselves alone one night, you exchange massive amounts of saliva. It was a harmless make out session, right? Kids being kids?

Consider these points:

1. She will never have a "first kiss" again. Shouldn't that have been something her future husband ought to have had, which can now never be given back?

We do not have to stretch our imagination very far to see further implications. Oral sex? Full intercourse? If you engage in these activities with a girl, you are taking that part of her sexual purity away from her. You cannot give it back to her. Was she a virgin? Not anymore. You took it from her. These are gifts that were meant for someone else which she is no longer able to give.

The problem is compounded once you leave her life. Now when she enters into other relationships, she has to have that awkward conversation with her other boyfriends. Or, years later she will have to tell her future husband of her past experiences, which you will be a part of, and perhaps your name will even come up. But kids will be kids, right?

What you take away from a young lady, whether it's the first kiss or her first time doing 'x' (touches included), you can never give back. At the same time, your sexual purity 'bowl' is being 'chipped.' The last thing you want to be carrying around is lots of sexual experiences with lots of different women. This will be baggage that you will regret having to carry. Be a 'husband of but one wife' by cultivating a proper approach to women now, even before you are married.

2. Secondly, consider also that in our harmless make out sessions we are creating an expectation of normalcy. I doubt anyone will dispute that media certainly conveys what it thinks is 'normal,' and 'making out' is almost always considered a normal beginning to an event that goes 'all the way.' Even with something that many will view as perfectly innocent, the expectation is created in the minds of both the boy and the girl that this is how relationships are *supposed* to work.

Now suppose a young woman begins dating someone who does *not* make out with her. What's her thought process? "Why isn't he making out with me? Am I not pretty enough? Does he not love me?" Vice versa, if you put the moves on her (as you think you are supposed to do) and she rejects your advances: "Am I not good enough for her? Why not? There must be something wrong with our relationship."

These may very well be conscious thoughts, but they might just as well arise in one's subconscious, pulling down the entire relationship. The more experiences you have, with more people, with increasing intensity, the more weight you put on future relationships. When the time comes when you think you have found the 'one,' you will find that this baggage will—consciously or subconsciously—carry over into this relationship, as well.

These are just some of the many unseen complexities and consequences of approaching sexuality and romance according to the standards of the world. We haven't even mentioned the possibility that one of your 'kids will be kids' moment might result in a new kid! You can avoid almost all of these difficulties by striving to maintain sexual purity for yourself and those you date, and align your conduct with God's expectations for you.

For a moment, set aside the prospect of having your behavior displease God. Just think about the different set of potential outcomes, here. On the one hand, there is the world's pattern, which ends up being a veritable train wreck for millions of people. On the other hand, there is God's pattern, which, if faithfully and diligently pursued, will generally leave not only the man and woman happier, but also their children. Seriously, in the end, God's way is just easier.

Romantic relationships are more than titles. Men and women who are involved in relationships are involved mentally, emotionally, physically and spiritually (MEPS).

As a young man it is your responsibility to protect all four of those areas—and that includes protecting the spirituality of the young woman you have taken an interest in. It is your task to lead in light of the cross of Christ, viewing her as a child of God, worthy of honor and dignity.

Certainly, being a child of God you will not abuse her physically. And because she is a child of God, bought and redeemed with the blood of Christ, violating her sexual purity (physical) should be the furthest thought from your mind. Get your hands off of her! She does not belong to you, she belongs to God. There is a time and a place for touching—after marriage.

We want to elevate the women, not bring them down to the world's standards and expectations. When we start our relationships at the cross (spiritual), our actions will reflect as much. And because we are treating the young lady appropriately, we can protect her emotions and thoughts, saving her from the pointless drama that all too often interferes with relationships.

Lead from the cross, not with your hormones. Leading from the cross means that we recognize our need for a Savior, we understand that our salvation comes from that Savior, and that our Savior has made us into a new creation. God has done a mighty thing in you, and has given you his Spirit to help you develop and protect that new creation—you *and* her.

So far, my emphasis has been on what we've learned from our parents growing up with an eye towards how sons will view women, based on how the father treated the mother and women in general. We have not even begun to talk about how your views of women will influence how your *daughter* views men. A father's love towards his wife will influence how the daughter views men, as well as romantic relationships more generally.

In my case, my son is the momma's boy and our daughter is daddy's little girl. She latches onto me as my son latches onto his mother. These are important relationships. However, my daughter does not latch onto me if I am distant from her mother and also distant from her. If I ignore her physically and emotionally, she will have an emotional and spiritual disconnect. This disconnect will continue with her as she progresses through life. If she does not receive the proper love and emotional support at home, she will go find it somewhere else.

I once knew this girl who felt she had such little value and worth that she turned to sex as a way to ease her pain. For her, having sex meant that she was 'loved.' In reality, they couldn't care less, just as long as they were getting some. She wasn't getting the right type of love and appreciation at home, so she looked elsewhere.

We can go on and on producing anecdotes and scenarios. We can drill down into numerous different ways that things can go wrong, or how they can go right. I'm not trying to judge anyone with any of the remarks so far, either. I've made my share of colossal blunders. Nonetheless, I want to clearly communicate that someday you will probably be a father, and as a father your attitudes and behaviors will influence both your son *and* your daughter. Those attitudes and behaviors are being shaped and manifested *right now.*

You will have to make a determination—now—as to whether or not you will view women as being made in God's image and have the utmost respect for them spiritually and emotionally by not violating them physically.

Perhaps you are wondering what exactly you can do now.

To begin with, if you are currently in a relationship you may very well want to sit down with your girlfriend and have a conversation about new boundaries, and why you are setting them. You should explain the rationale for the boundaries, or as I mentioned before, they may interpret what is happening as there being something wrong with them, or wrong with the relationship.

More generally, you can set your own spiritual boundaries and not cross them. What might those boundaries be? Open up your Bible and read it. Search out some good books that are recommended as having godly counsel. It might require effort but it isn't brain surgery, either. Hints: Those who treat women with respect don't grope, fondle, or make out with them; those who do open doors for them, speak words of affirmation to them, and respect their parents. You see where I'm going.

My students always ask me when I will have "the talk" with my children. From what I have said so far, you won't be surprised to learn that I respond, "When they are born." Likewise, you ought to lead by example and be overly intentional in viewing women properly, so that the example you set for your children is a godly one.

Godly men view women in light of the Redemptive Cross and love them as much as Christ loved the church.

Will you lead your significant other to the cross or way from it?

Will your son lead their wives and children
towards Christ, or away from him?

What I tell the young ladies:

Young ladies, look at the young man's past. Is it filled with broken hearts and failed promises? Is he more interested in placing his hands on your body than he is in placing God's word into your heart? If he is more interested in bumping and grinding on the dance floor, he certainly is not interested in respecting you as a young woman who belongs to God. If he's all over the girls... he'll be over you quickly.

Chapter 6

Mental Vigilance

Now the overseer is to be above reproach, faithful to his wife, **temperate,** self-controlled, respectable, hospitable, able to teach, not given to drunkenness, not violent but gentle, not quarrelsome, not a lover of money.

Temperate

Greek word: νεφαλεος
Transliterated: Nephaleos

Pronounced: nay-fal'-eh-os

Many translations of the Greek word νεφαλεος use the word "temperate" to convey its meaning. The word carries with it the meaning of abstaining from wine or moderate usage. The King James Version renders it as "vigilant." If you have been intoxicated before, even a little, the KJV choice will make more sense to you. As one becomes more and more intoxicated, one's awareness of his surroundings become dull until at last it is completely gone. Without awareness, you can't possibly be "vigilant." However, since Paul already makes explicit mention to drunkenness just a few words later, it does not seem that Paul has alcohol in mind quite yet. Instead, the context seems more to do with 'being of right mind, or vigilant and mentally aware and on guard.'

A godly man, then, is one who is above reproach, faithful to his wife, being mentally aware and on guard, being able to control his mind as well as his actions.

When I saw the King James Version using "vigilant" and did a little reading on the usage, I instantly thought back to my years growing up.

One occasion in particular stands out. While home alone, I decided to move one of our vehicles to a better location in our driveway. At just that moment, I noticed a beat-up, white work truck turned into the driveway. "Perhaps," I thought to myself, "the van is simply using our driveway to turn around." However, our driveway was relatively long. He certainly didn't need to use the whole thing, if that was what he wanted to do. I mentally ruled out other innocent explanations for him being in our driveway as he slowly crept towards the house, getting closer…. closer…. closer…

What to do? Quickly, I pumped the brake lights letting them know someone was in the car. They stopped. I ran inside the house, grabbed the shot gun and was ready to roll. The van backed out of the driveway and I never saw it again. A few days later, I heard that a white van was left abandoned a few homes down from our house, which drew the attention of the local police department. Vigilance, perhaps, had saved my life.

The point of this story should be obvious: We should be on our guard, vigilant and aware of our surroundings and more importantly the teachings and beliefs that surround us. An overseer of his family, but also his congregation, should be on guard and vigilant. If you are buzzed with alcohol or the world, you cannot see or think clearly, because your thinking is clouded. If a danger suddenly materializes, you will not fare well. Both your body and your mind are compromised. Conversely, someone who is sober and clear minded can see and think clearly and take appropriate action.

Being sober and clear minded is especially important for newly graduated young men and women heading off to college!

They will be leaving behind their parents, established friends, the security and comfort of home, and likely, opportunities for daily worship and reflection of God's Word. While the transition from high school to college is exciting, it also makes young men and women more vulnerable than they were previously. Freedom knocks at every door. Combining copious amounts of freedom and spiritual vulnerability with the mental and emotional rollercoaster of the first few weeks of college, it becomes even more important to be mentally, emotionally, physically and spiritually (especially!) vigilant.

I see it as one of my primary responsibilities as an educator to make my students aware that they are stepping into a new and exciting, yet dangerous transition. Once they graduate, they will find that their faith will be challenged in various ways. If they go to college, they might expect that their professors will call them out for being Christian in front of everyone else. Although such things are obviously possible, I tell them I do not think that will be their experience. I tell them that I think the greatest challenge to their faith will emerge on a different front.

I give them this quote: "The greatest challenge to your faith is going to be the subtleties of life."

I tell them some of the most significant challenges to their faith are the seemingly innocuous decisions we make daily. Most of them won't ever experience a dramatic confrontation with someone hostile to their faith, but they will have countless smaller experiences which, if not guarded against, could weaken one's faith a great deal.

Given the wide variety of experiences each of us have every day, most of them believed to be fairly innocent, I can't possibly lay them all out for your consideration. So, let me take just one example where something often taken for granted as representing no danger at all could add up to big problems over time.

Music.

Music influences the mind significantly. It relates, motivates, soothes, and entertains the listener. The reason we listen to music is because we know it influences us. We *want* the influence. Given this, it should follow that we ought to be on our guard against that within music which could influence us in negative ways. Unfortunately, much of the music we listen to has little to do with the new creation we have in Christ. Given this, it should follow that we ought to be on our guard against that within music which not only could influence us negatively, but contradicts who we say we are, and our beliefs.

Carefully read Ephesians 5:

> But among you there must not be even a hint of sexual immorality, or of any kind of impurity, or of greed, because these are improper for God's holy people. Nor should there be obscenity, foolish talk or coarse joking, which are out of place, but rather thanksgiving. For of this you can be sure: No immoral, impure or greedy person—such a person is an idolater—has any inheritance in the kingdom of Christ and of God. Let no one deceive you with empty words, for because of such things God's wrath comes on those who are disobedient. Therefore, do not be partners with them.

How does the music you listen to compare with the encouragement Paul offers the Ephesians?

Some people object that music does not 'influence' us. Those who really believe that are being naive. Most who say that, however, are not being honest. As I said, if the music did not exert some influence on us, in some way, why would we listen to it at all?

It is just a fact that music influences not only our mood *but our beliefs as well.*

The producers and artist are not naive about this fact, but many of us are! Really, everyone knows it, except those who want to justify listening to music which contradicts their own beliefs.

Think about another example where people deny that any influence is happening: television commercials. If a commercial did not help sell the product, then why is the business paying for it? Are we to believe that all of these companies are going to spend millions and millions of dollars on something they do not reasonably expect will make them money? Seriously.

The common response is, "Does it really matter?" Yes, yes it does. The lessons being taught in much of the music we listen to is contrary to the teachings of Christ and Scripture. It seems harmless, like it's no big deal and we act as though it has no influence, but that is only because we have not been vigilant. We have not taken captive every thought to make it obedient to Christ. We have not thought of those things which are true, right, noble, pure, excellent, praiseworthy, or admirable (Philippians 4).

I mentioned commercials, but of course television is no different. What we watch influences our beliefs. Much of it serves to erode the Truth. The majority of what is on television has little to do with anything holy. It's small, it's subtle, and seems harmless; then again, a small amount of lead seems harmless, too. But then one day there is enough lead in your body where the harm becomes impossible to ignore.

I have given the examples of music and television because of their obvious ability to shape attitudes over time while be seemingly benign all along. However, how we entertain ourselves is just one small slice of our daily experience. If it was something starkly opposed to our faith, we'd instantly see the danger it presented, and act accordingly. But, in the subtleties of life, its moments, decisions, and experiences, we let our guard down. The danger does not appear imminent. It is easy to pay little or no attention to these small parts of our lives. I argue that it is just in these moments, where we think things are so safe that it is not even worth keeping guard anymore, that are some of the greatest threats to our faith.

Paul is aware of this. That is why he expects an overseer to be vigilant, on guard, and thinking clearly. In our world of "pick your own truth," being vigilant is important.

In Acts 20, Paul encourages the Ephesians to be vigilant when he wrote:

> Keep watch over yourselves and all the flock of which the Holy Spirit has made you overseers. Be shepherds of the church of God, which he bought with his own blood. I know that after I leave, savage wolves will come in among you and will not spare the flock. Even from your own number men will arise and distort the truth in order to draw away disciples after them. So be on your guard!

He knows this is the last time he will see the Ephesians. He warns them that wolves will come in, Christian wolves perhaps, and distort the truth. That is scary, but it's true. How many of our Christian friends and family are actually leading us away from the faith due to their practices and their beliefs? Are you on guard? What you are exposing yourself to? Are you being vigilant and paying attention to what you are putting into your mind?

If not, you are making yourself extremely vulnerable to the hollow and deceptive philosophies of the world, which are based on human tradition as opposed to Christ (Colossians 2:8).

Are you standing at the door, ready for action? Are you standing vigilant in the faith, so that you may grow in his Word? Or is your mind cloudy, and buzzing with the philosophies of the world and the lies being taught, sometimes even by Christians and congregations?

Stand firm, take captive every thought, and be vigilant.

What I tell the young ladies:

Is the young man you are dating or want to date more interested in the world, or the Word? His actions speak volumes as to whether or not he is going to lead you in Christ or lead you according to the world. If his words and beliefs are contrary to the Word of God, you can be sure he has not taken the time to consider being vigilant against worldly philosophies. It seems harmless, but this is the man who is going to be leading you...either towards the cross or away from it. If you marry him, you can expect that influence to continue to add up over time, leading you to possibly adopt attitudes that you would abhor, if you considered them in light of the Scriptures.

Chapter 7

Relax, Dude.

> Now the overseer is to be above reproach, faithful to his wife, temperate, **self-controlled**, respectable, hospitable, able to teach, not given to drunkenness, not violent but gentle, not quarrelsome, not a lover of money.

Self-Controlled

Greek word: σοφρον
Transliterated: Sophron

Pronounced: so'-frone

Paul characterizes godliness as not being violent, but being gentle, temperate and self-controlled. Control of one's mental faculties results in control of one's physical actions, so goes the reasoning. If one cannot control his mind, controlling his actions will be even more difficult.

There are plenty of examples to go around, some already listed on the previous and proceeding pages. There was a time in my life when I had felt like I had limited control over my mind. My thoughts seemed like they were being planted from an outside source. I would often ask myself, and even to this day, "Why am I thinking this?" The thoughts did not make any sense with who I was or who I professed to be. More so out of confusion than anything else, I went to see a psychologist. Initially I had thought I was clinically depressed because I was relatively moody and often just "down." As I look back at those years, I disagree with my self-diagnosis.

I am not convinced I was depressed; I think I lacked contentment. I did not have any real purpose and meaning other than to survive each day teaching. There was a larger purpose of course for the Kingdom, but I am not sure how committed I was to that purpose. Without being anchored to my convictions, my thoughts wavered and overwhelmed me. Eventually I was able to take control of my thoughts, which is why today I am not convinced that I was depressed, but rather lacked contentment with who I am and what my existence was on a daily basis.

Once that realization happened, I became content and satisfied, with Brian Horvath. It has taken me years to come to that conclusion, but it has arrived. We will read more about maintaining mental self-control later.

One of the first examples I thought of when reading about self-control was driving and the various responses we have to other drivers. If there is one area where many people lack self-control, it is driving. It happens to us all. We are driving and minding our own business when the driver in front of us immediately turns without using the signal. This causes us to have to slam on the breaks or swerve out of the way. Easy response, right? Just keep on driving while ignoring the idiocy in front of you! Well, rather than ignoring the problem, we often see drivers retaliate with inappropriate hand gestures, which can sometimes escalate.

At Lutheran North, where I teach, we have chapel four times a week. Each day before chapel there are announcements read to the entire school. Many students pay attention during this time, while many also talk through it. Personally, I find it disrespectful when someone chatters through the announcements. In front of us is an individual who is trying to communicate to the student body important information, and they can't control themselves long enough to receive that information. Given how many other times people have to chit-chat, you'd think muzzling themselves for a few minutes wouldn't be so difficult. Apparently, it is.

While I have a low view of disrespect in any capacity, this is admittedly a minor example. However, remember in the last section where I argued that the real dangers to our spirituality manifest in such minor matter. If you can't control yourself when it is relatively easy to do so, why would you think you'll be able to control yourself when faced with an escalated situation?

We have already seen where self-control would be important in athletics. Referees and umpires are humans. They do not always make the correct decision, or the decision you agree with. You can see where this is going. Parents, players, and coaches go ballistic. Yelling and screaming at the referee because they didn't get their way.

Sure, at times, coaches need to protect their players. Yet, one does not have to lose their mind or dignity. I thought it was a good example of where we are at in society when a player thanked me for getting after a referee for a bad call. I had apparently not responded how he wanted me to respond over the years and finally, after all of this time, I had finally "manned up" and gave it to the referee.

Granted, I still did it with self-control, but my point is that I was actually commended for drawing closer to 'flying off the handle.'

One of the definitions of the Greek word σωϖφρων (self-control) is "curbing one's desires and impulses."

Look at our examples again. You are on the road and driver in front of you turns unexpectedly. Your impulse is to flick the driver off, cuss through the rolled up window, or blare your horn. Why? What does cussing at the person who has already turned down a different street accomplish? Your blood boils over and now you are angry. Consider the circumstances. You are alive. You had to swerve out of the way. I get that, but you are alive.

You have a choice in those moments: To control your desire to rip into the person, or to give into your impulses. Sometimes, honking the horn is necessary, especially if the person is merging into your lane and he fails to see you are in the same lane! So you honk your horn, letting them know you are there, and you move on. The other option is you honk your horn, change lanes, lay on your horn again and stare the person down…because you are going to do what exactly? You are alive. For now! If this escalates, maybe not so much.

This took me a while to learn but it came when I started to learn mental self-control. When I learned to control my impulses and my desires, road rage became less of an issue. I am alive. I am certainly not going to let someone on the road who is clueless (for whatever reason that you really don't know) ruin my attitude and day all because he did not use his turn signal. Frankly, I really cannot afford to lose my control. We have already talked about the influence we have on other people. Children pick up on every action and word parents do and say. The example I set for my children in the car will be followed.

Chapel is little different. People talk when they are not supposed to because they have the impulse to talk. Their desire to talk to their neighbor is greater than the respect they have for the person speaking. It is an easy choice. Do not talk. How hard can it be? Understand the situation and save the conversation for later. Is what you are talking about so important that you cannot wait? Is it really so important that it is worth disrespecting the person speaking? What might it say to others if you are observed being disrespectful? What might it say to others if you are observed being respectful?

So, the referee made a bad call. You move on. You ignore it. As a player, you let the coach take care of it. In a recent playoff game, we had two players both receive yellow cards in the first five minutes of the game. Why? They could not keep silent. Because of their lack of self-control, I had to pull them off the field for the time being. Were they a greater help to their team on the field, or mouthing off and now riding the bench? Near the end of the game, the referee made another controversial call. Their response was the same. This time, they received red cards and were out the rest of the game. Now their team was really paying the consequences for their inability to stay quiet. Unfortunately, instead of letting the coaches take care of it, they lacked the ability to control themselves and it put the team down to nine players against eleven.

These are all basic examples of self-control and controlling our impulses. But if we are not vigilant and aware of our surroundings, of what we are doing and *how* we are doing it, it's pretty easy to lack self-control. Self-control requires discipline. Discipline takes effort. We certainly cannot have pastors who are unable to control their impulses or desires. If we are talking about what it looks like to be a godly man, we definitely cannot have young Christian men who are unable to control their impulses and desires. We have already discussed numerous examples where having self-control would have saved one's integrity, honor, and dignity.

It would be a mistake to look at these three examples and wave them away as being inconsequential. Don't forget what I said! "The greatest challenge to your faith is going to be the subtleties of life." Although I think they are valid in themselves, if you wanted, you could think of these 'inconsequential' situations as being practice for more serious and urgent situations which will surely arise in your life. As you train, so you will perform. If you lack self-control in the small things, it will be harder to exert it in the big things.

And, mark my words, there will be big things to come.

Who is in control? You, or your emotions?

What I tell the young ladies:

If your boyfriend plays console games (PS2/Xbox), pay attention to how he deals with failure. If he cusses, swears, or throws controllers or anything else when he loses, these may be warning signs of an abusive personality. Does he have road rage? Does he talk bad about people behind their back when he is angry? If he cannot control himself with others, what makes you so sure he'll be able to control himself with *you?*

Chapter 8

Be Respect

> Now the overseer is to be above reproach, faithful to his wife, temperate, self-controlled, **respectable**, hospitable, able to teach, not given to drunkenness, not violent but gentle, not quarrelsome, not a lover of money.

Respectable

Greek word: κοσμιος
Transliterated: kosmios

Pronounced: kos'-mee-os

The majority of translations translate the Greek word κοσμιος as "respectable." It also means "modest." Below are a few of the different translation of the same verse.

NASB: An overseer, then, must be above reproach, the husband of one wife, temperate, prudent, respectable, hospitable, able to teach...

NIV: Now the overseer is to be above reproach, faithful to his wife, temperate, self-controlled, respectable, hospitable, able to teach...

KVJ: A bishop then must be blameless, the husband of one wife, vigilant, sober, of good behavior, given to hospitality, apt to teach...

ASV: The bishop therefore must be without reproach, the husband of one wife, temperate, sober-minded, orderly, given to hospitality, apt to teach...

Our actions, thoughts, and words are all to align if we wish to be considered respectable.

I cannot tell you how many times in the course of almost twenty years of teaching, that I have seen students behave disrespectfully, only to see their friends give them props. How embarrassing is it that for someone to get respect from others and to respect themselves, they have to disrespect others?

I was a 9th grader at Lutheran Westland in Michigan. My next class was men's choir. Oh, how I dreaded that class. I was an athlete, not a singer. I had no desire to learn how to sing, nor was I comfortable singing in front of people. Even today I will not do karaoke. As I have aged, I have wanted to learn how to sing. Add it to my bucket list. This particular day in choir I was moving with lightning speed to class. The room had built in risers. I'm not sure why but I ran up the right side of the room to the top of the risers. My intention was to make it to the other side of the room. I was in full speed when a sophomore who was lying up against the back wall with his friend raised his legs and tripped me. I wiped out hard. The result was my complete humiliation and embarrassment. What did he receive? A high five from his friends.

Stories such as these are not unique to me. They happen every day in high school and college. Young men are proud of their disrespect towards others. I am in the camp that believes that parents today are more interested in being friends with their children than parenting them. Thus, there is an epidemic of lack of respect in the world today. 'Friends' high five disrespect—parents call out the disrespect in their own children!

What does being respectable look like for you today? We will look at it from a couple different perspectives. One will be respectable behavior and the other will be respectable words.

My high school coaches and teachers would likely agree that I did not disrupt class or act in a way that was disrespectful to them. I was brought up properly to respect authority. Granted, I did not pay attention in class as much as I should have, but I did not disrupt nor did I mouth off. The consequences for being rude and disrespectful towards a teacher would have been greater at home than those received at school.

I knew enough to not talk back to my parents. I did that one time in high school and my mother justifiably smacked me across the face. While I am obviously against child abuse, I support disciplining a child. I suspect most people would contend that it is only natural that a young man challenges their parents. It is all "biological" or "part of growing up," they might say.

This probably explains why so many young men disrespect their parents, teachers, and other authority figures. They do not fear their parents because their parents will not discipline their children sternly, evidently because the parents fear the child.

Should you be the parent of your child, or the child's friend? I wonder where you stand. This is what the Scriptures say:

Ephesians 6: 1-2: "Children, obey your parents in the Lord, for this is right. Honor your father and mother, which is the first commandment with a promise..."

Colossians 3:20: "Children, obey your parents in everything, for this pleases the Lord."

In which ways do you openly and deliberately *respect* your parents? Notice we did not say *disrespect* but respect. When your parents ask you to do something, do you do it? When do you do it? Do you make excuses? Do you "forget?"

This one definitely relates to me as a teacher and a parent. You can easily tell which students have it easier at home with responsibility. As a teacher I will ask a student to accomplish a specific task, whatever it may be, and the student will respond with something that will preclude him or her from doing that task at that moment. There is always an excuse and it is always expected that the excuse will be honored. They don't get this idea out of thin air.

Like many high schools, our school has a dress code which expects the students to have their shirts tucked in. This of course causes contention, because according to the student body, it is an absurd request to have to tuck your shirt in. I wonder what these same students will do when they go off to work and their employer will expect them to have their shirts tucked in—gasp!—they may even have to wear a tie. Almost every time I ask students to tuck their shirts in they give the same excuses. One of the most common excuses is: "I just got out of PE." How is that relevant? I didn't ask where you came from or where you were going. I asked you politely to tuck your shirt in. They are so conditioned to making excuses it has become natural to them.

Another common response is when you ask a student (or athlete) to complete "x" task and they respond that they are doing something else. I have had enough of that over the years. You should see the looks I get when I expect my students/athletes to actually do some type of manual labor that requires that they stop whatever they are doing. My own children try to do the same thing at home. I'll ask them to clean up their toys and they will respond with "Well, I'm doing 'x' right now..." In which I respond, politely, with, "Please do what you have been asked to do, *now*." You see, I do not want my children to be the kind of young man or woman where, when asked to do something at school or the work place, they make excuses or tell their boss to kiss off, because they perceive that what they are doing is more important than what was asked of them.

It probably does not seem obvious to many, but listening to authority figures is a manifestation of being respectful. Are you typically arguing with your parents? Do you typically make excuses or try to justify your behavior even when you know it is wrong? Part of being a respectable young man is doing that which is asked of you, with integrity, and without excuse.

I even see parents justifying their child's behavior. When the parents find excuses for the child's decisions, the child learns that whatever has happened is never his fault or responsibility. As a consequence, the blame is shifted to the coaches, teachers, or law enforcement officers. While this may be an effective tactic in the short term, in the long term it is inevitable that something happens which is undeniably your responsibility. If you are not used to owning up to your own decisions by then, this could be an extremely uncomfortable experience.

Making out with girls is not respectable behavior. Staying at a girl's house past hours is not respectable behavior. Cuddling with my girlfriend in her mother's house was not respecting her mother or my girlfriend. Part of being a respectable person is respecting other people and who they are. It is not elevating yourself and your wants above the interests of others, especially, but not exclusively, when it is they who have the right to have their interests honored.

As a teenager, I spent many hours being bored. That's a dangerous mixture: bored as a teenager. My friends and I were driving around the town and managed to find some yard decorations which they smashed while I drove and allowed it to happen. To this day, I have no idea why we did that. Being bored, I remembered trying to smash someone's mailbox. Why? How arrogant and disrespectful do you have to be to destroy someone else's property? In 2016, my wife and I had left out two full bowls of Halloween candy on the porch. Our video cameras caught a young man running up to the porch grabbing not only the candy, but the bowls as well! I was disappointed but I also laughed. I could not be too upset considering the stupidity and disrespectful actions I participated in when I was a young lad. Yet, it is in the subtle things in life where problematic habits and attitudes develop and manifest.

Hopefully you have not intentionally destroyed someone's

property. But what about at home and at school? Are you the kind that instead of walking twenty feet to the trash, you drop your trash on the floor? Do you throw your trash out of the car window instead of waiting to get home? Destroying someone's property physically or simply throwing or leaving your trash out is a sign of disrespect. It means you think you and your time or property is more important than the interests, time, and property of others.

Romans 12:3:

> For by the grace given me I say to every one of you: Do not think of yourself more highly than you ought, but rather think of yourself with sober judgment, in accordance with the faith God has distributed to each of you.

And Philippians 2:3:

> Do nothing out of selfish ambition or vain conceit. Rather, in humility value others above yourselves...

Romans 12:3 and Philippians 2:3 represent a type of attitude we should have towards other people—not in order to be saved, but just because it is right and good to be respectful towards others. In order to respect others, you cannot be arrogant and self-centered. If you think you are the king of the earth, then you definitely will not treat people in a way that reflects who they are in the King of Christ.

You can see in Romans 12 that we are all are in the same spot: sinful, separated from God, and therefore, none of us should think of ourselves more highly than we ought. We are all the same: Saved by God just like they are saved by God's grace. God didn't have to save us, but he did. Thus, elevating ourselves above others and treating others below us is definitely not respectable behavior. When we disrespect others, we disrespect the one who saved all.

To be respectable, we need to have humility and understand our place. I remember trying to encourage this humility in my soccer athletes. I know they perceived it as me trying to grab power and exert my authority over them, but that was not the case. Understanding the sincere lack of disrespect in the world, I wanted to encourage them to be overly respectful. I wanted them to go above and beyond modern expectations about politeness. I expected them to say, "Yes, Sir," and, "Yes, Ma'am."

I didn't think it was unreasonable, but like I said, I think they laughed at the idea and thought my motives were different. In reality, I just wanted them to *be* respect.

My mother tried the same thing when I was in high school, which was around the same time she had opened her own martial arts dojo. If you ever hear me say that my mother can beat up your dad, I'm not lying. She probably can!

In the martial arts world, it is assumed that you give your instructor the utmost respect. You do so not because they are the authority figure and you should respect them because they say so. No, you respect them because you understand and appreciate where they have come from and what they have done to grow themselves, which places them in a better position to help you. When you say, "Yes, Sir," you are essentially saying, "You have more martial arts experience than I do. You know more. I know you know more and I'm ready to listen to you, Sir."

There is great humility in such language and having that type of attitude. You verbally acknowledge that you do not know what you do not know. You are admitting to not being "all that." That is hard to do as a young man. As young men, we think we know and can do almost anything. If I know everything and can do almost anything, why would I listen to anyone else?

Well, when you say, "Yes, Sir," or, "Yes, Ma'am," you are in "humility in value(ing) others above yourselves," and "not thinking of yourself more highly than you ought" (Philippians 2:3). Often times when I speak to my elders this way, they will respond with a quick, "Do not call me 'Sir.'" I think some people equate it to being called, "old," when in reality it's simply recognition that all people deserve the highest level of respect.

Well, as you might suspect, when my mother tried to get me, a high school teenager, to show due respect, there was no way I was going to submit. I saw it as a power grab. I was not going to do it. Looking back, I suspect she was motivated by the same desire that motivated me to expect my players to speak with the utmost respect: she simply wanted to instill respect in her son.

My players didn't do it when I asked them to do it either. I don't blame them. We started off strong the first day, but it did not take very long for players to stop following through with the request. I did not make a big deal out of it, though. Respectful humility is important to the success of the program, but not to the point where I was going to punish them for not saying what I wanted them to say.

Forced respect isn't really respect at all. Even though it didn't 'take,' I think it was good for my players to at least see an example of what giving respect might look like.

Do you treat people and value people more than they value themselves? When you speak to people, do you talk down to them? Or do you speak up to them?

Our actions, thoughts, and words are all to align if we wish to be considered respectable. When these three are aligned we become respectable. 1 Timothy 3:7 declares, "He must also have a good reputation with outsiders, so that he will not fall into disgrace and into the devil's trap."

When our actions, thoughts, and words are aligned and manifest spiritual fruits, not only are we respectful individuals but we are also respectable. If an outsider sees a Christian leader treating others with disrespect, the leader's message will not be taken seriously. If a Christian leader is seen getting drunk on the weekends (or weekdays), then the person's reputation is trashed. No one is going to listen to them. Their words will carry only so much weight.

We all know that when someone's actions do not match their words, the person's reputation is tarnished. We could easily dismiss 'respectable' as only applying to bishops and leaders because they are the face of the Christian church, but that would ignore what was said in the previous chapters: *you* are a leader of the Christian church, even if you did not or are not going to the seminary.

There are positive consequences from showing respect, but the consequences are not often immediate. They reveal themselves over time. (The same is entirely true of showing disrespect.) For example, a day will come when you may want letters of recommendations written. You will want to use a teacher or a coach as a referral. Scholarship applications will be filled out, asking you to provide references. Facebook profiles will be read. Employers will assess your handshake or lack of handshake. They will see your manners, or lack of manners. The fruit of your previous behavior will be used to judge whether or not you are a respectable person. You will be a 'face' of their product. Even if you sit in a cubicle every day, you will be expected to treat your co-workers and customers in a way

> **Pro Tip:** If you come to me and ask me to write a letter of recommendation, but everything about you is not respectful or respectable, I will not write the letter of recommendation for you.

which best represents the company and product. Your employers understand this, even if you do not yet, at present.

As I found out, you can easily demand respect and get respect—although the significance of it will not be equal to the level of respect you will get if you earn the respect by your very own actions, thoughts, and words.

If you think this topic of respect is a small one, you are greatly mistaken. The next time you talk to another man, look him in the eyes, shake his hand, and say, "Good Morning, Sir." Pay attention to what follows. When you talk to the parents of your girlfriend and refer to them as "Sir" and "Ma'am" and endeavor to go above and beyond their expectations, take note of their reaction. When you are employed, do the same thing. Say "Sir" and "Ma'am" but also go above and beyond their expectations, without being prompted by them to do so. Observe the results.

When we are disrespectful, when we elevate ourselves above other people and their property, we not only lose out on opportunities to network, but more importantly we lose out on opportunities to grow as people. Worse, when we are not respectful and respectable, we misrepresent the image of God and the love he has for others.

Respect the moment you are in and the people in those moments with you. When you do this, you become a respectable and respectful person. Respectable and respectful people are of great value to families, teams, educational institutions, and places of employment. They know this, even if you do not, yet. Yet. One day, you will learn, for better or for worse, what follows from being respectful and what follows from being disrespectful.

One of the last comments we will make will be focused on the promise referred to in Ephesians 6. The promise stems from Deuteronomy 5 which says,

> Honor your father and your mother, as the LORD your God has commanded you, so that you may live long and that it may go well with you in the land the LORD your God is giving you.

Even if you aren't a Christian, this command makes obvious sense. Even if you don't like taking orders from an 'old' book, there is wisdom in this passage. Even without doing an intensive study on "so that you may live long and that it may go well with you in the land…" we can see benefits of honoring and respecting your parents.

It is not hard to figure out.

Look, if your parents tell you to not run in the middle of the road while traffic is whizzing by, it would be wise to respect their prudent request. Failure to respect their wishes may very well result in *your death*. When a teacher asks you to tuck your shirt in, or "x," do it. Ok, you're probably not going to be run over by a truck while walking down the school hallway, although you might get a detention if you decide to flaunt the request. Setting aside the fear of punishment, it is still wise to respect your teacher's prudent request. The benefits may not be immediately seen but will bear fruit over time and manifest in unexpected ways. Like your parents, your coaches and teachers and other 'authority' figures have been around for awhile. They have seen the dangers of life and have insight on how to enjoy the rewards. When you show respect for others, you may be saving yourself. When you show respect for others, you are respecting your future self. Think about that.

Honor your father and mother by providing them a high level of respect. Honor your coaches, teachers, and employers. They have more knowledge and experience than you do. This knowledge and experience can help you grow as a person and also keep you safe. There are so many seen and unseen consequences to actions that it is worth your humility. Authority figures have been given to you, to help you. God has entrusted you to their care. By title alone, they are looking out for your best interest. Sure, people abuse that position of authority, but that does not warrant disrespect.

Consider others and the position they hold over you as an opportunity for you. View them as servants, not as oppressors. Lift them up. Honor them.

Choose wisely.

Are you simply checking the "respect" box off for the sake of playing time or being in the good graces of another person?

Or are you being respectful because you yourself *are* respect?

What I tell the young ladies:

Does he trash people when they aren't around? Is he cheating on his homework in front of you? Is he breaking the curfew set by his or your parents? Is he lying to your parents or making excuses as to why he brought you home late? Is he staying at your house later than he should? A young, worldly man is going to be easy to spot. He will lack respect for himself and for others. You don't want to be around when the bill comes due.

Chapter 9

Love Your Neighbor Selflessly

> Now the overseer is to be above reproach, faithful to his wife, temperate, self-controlled, respectable, **hospitable**, able to teach, not given to drunkenness, not violent but gentle, not quarrelsome, not a lover of money.

Hospitable

Greek word: φιλοξενος
Transliterated: Philoxenos

Pronounced: fil-ox'-en-os

Probably one of the most challenging books I have read was Shane Claiborne's *Irresistible Revolution.* It documents his unconditional love towards other people, illustrated for example by him moving in and living with homeless people and building a community with them. There I was as a young man, all of thirty years old, reading about a type of Christianity I was not familiar with—a type of Christianity undoubtedly lived by the first century Christians. I was literally floored in tears at my selfishness, but also being moved into empathy with the brokenhearted.

I was coming home from work and I saw a homeless man. I stepped outside of my comfort box and pulled my car over next to him as he was walking. I asked him if he wanted food, which of course, he said he did. He hopped in the car and I drove him to Little Caesars where I bought him a pizza. A few hesitant and intense miles later, I dropped him off at his next location. And that was that. I went home. I had done my good deed.

I was contemplating the significance of what had just happened. A wave of empathy hit me. Here was this guy who was homeless for years, out on the streets and disconnected from his family for what I understood to be over twenty years. And then there was me, sitting in a nice warm bath, a loaded fridge, and access to my family and friends whenever I wanted. I was under the impression that he was rather comfortable with his existence. Perhaps I was more disappointed by his situation than he was. That didn't matter. That was about him and this was about me.

Paul uses the same words in 1 Timothy 3 that he does when

writing Titus 1:7. In Titus 1:8, Paul writes, "Rather, he must be hospitable, one who loves what is good, who is self-controlled, upright, holy and disciplined." The meaning and application of his words is obvious: being generous to guests.

It would have been especially important in the first century for a pastor to be hospitable. The Christians in the first century were anything but popular. Unfortunately, opponents of Christians were *not* hospitable. They certainly were not being generous to guests. In AD 64 there was a fire in Rome. Nero, according to Tacitus, blames the Christians. To punish them, Nero lit the Christians on fire and used them as torches in his garden. It was so gruesome that even some of the Romans were offended (*Annals of Rome,* Tacitus).

The persecution of Christians began almost immediately after the birth of Christianity, and forced Christians to be careful. They worshipped in their homes. It is quite possible that Christians were displaced and needed places to hide. In this context, it only makes sense that Paul would go out of his way to insist that an overseer of other Christians be hospitable, entertaining, and generous to guests.

Being hospitable, regardless of whether or not a person is a Christian, aligns itself with the Gospel of Christ. Christ has a history of being generous to his guests, *us*. While he could easily turn us away, he, like the father welcoming the prodigal son back, opens his arms and embraces us.

I had embraced the homeless man so far as to buy him some food. I wondered, though, if I had enough courage to invite him into the home, for a shower and a full meal. What I failed to do, Christ did. His sacrifice on our behalf makes us eligible to come into the Father's Home and have full access to the banquet table.

It is this love that compels us to love others. It is the love that moved Shane Claiborne to take the leap of faith that he did. It is the same generosity towards others that a new creation in Christ exhibits. We don't do it for reward, but because Christ's love lives in us. If Christ's love lives in us, it is only natural to have that love flow out of His new creation.

It baffles me that Christians miss this point. While we live in a divisive world, there is no excuse for hatred. A Christian can certainly disagree morally or even politically with someone, but denying them the same love that Christ gave that same person is absurd. Who am I to not love the one whom God has loved?

This is another conversation that routinely comes up in my

classes. What is love? And to what extent do we as Christians show that love to others?

1 John 3 is convicting. If it is not, we misunderstand the Gospel. Here it is:

> This is how we know what love is: Jesus Christ laid down his life for us. And we ought to lay down our lives for our brothers and sisters. If anyone has material possessions and sees a brother or sister in need but has no pity on them, how can the love of God be in that person? Dear children, let us not love with words or speech but with actions and in truth.

Confused? I am not sure how you could be. If anyone has material possessions and does not have pity, how in the world could God's love be in that person?

True story: We were having this conversation in class and a student shrugged it off and claimed that homeless people were outside of their responsibility. In essence, the student's words and demeanor were such that he was saying that those in that situation were filthy and unworthy of love. Explain to me how a Christian who has the grace of God given to them freely pushes off the responsibility of loving our neighbors? The student was not even arguing that it was unsafe to help a homeless person. They simply contended they were not worth their time and resources.

I suspect that the student has had a change of heart. Many students do once they leave the cozy existence of an upper to middle class environment. Nonetheless, there are still millions of Christians who ignore the opportunity to be generous to strangers and even their own families!

Related to the discussion is 1 John 4:19-21:

> We love because he first loved us. Whoever claims to love God yet hates a brother or sister is a liar. For whoever does not love their brother and sister, whom they have seen, cannot love God, whom they have not seen. And he has given us this command: Anyone who loves God must also love their brother and sister.

And yet another swift kick to the gut.

I hear young Christian men and women state they hate such and such person all of the time. Sure, sometimes it is joking. Other times it is very serious. That's a serious concern. Again, we have young Christian men who have the grace of God, declaring and showing obvious hatred towards other Christians. We don't get it. If we truly hate someone, we truly do not have God's love in us. How could we? An existence of hatred is one of the flesh and not of the Spirit. Those who have fellowship with the flesh and darkness do not have fellowship with the light (1 John 1).

Christians are expected to be generous and love other people, not out of fear or because we are seeking a reward, but because Christ first loved us.

If you are missing this point, you are missing the heart of Christianity: Christ's unconditional, unwarranted love for you. It's a gift to you and it is to be a gift to others. Christ is using *you* to give that same love to others, regardless of the person standing in front of you at a given moment.

There are many practical manifestations of this love if you are vigilant. At times the opportunities will easily present themselves.

A classic example is the car that has stalled in the middle of the road. Their hazard lights are on and every car is doing their best to avoid their schedules being interrupted. One option comes easily to the mind: get out of your car and help push the car to a safe spot, out of the road. Offer further assistance in the form of a cell phone, a ride to the gas station, or simply offer to wait with them while help arrives. This can be tricky at times because you may have a passenger or it may be dark out. You certainly need to be prudent. Often, pulling your car into an adjacent parking lot and walking out to the car is your best bet.

A less dangerous example is simply buying a stranger food. We hear these stories on the news. There isn't anything holding us back from such things except an attachment to our money. There is no need to make a big deal out of the purchase. Quietly tell the cashier you are purchasing the food for the individuals behind or in front of you, and move on. Why? You can. That's why. If you are a student, go out of your way to pray with another student or teacher. Do not ask for a request and then walk away. Pray with them, right there.

Even if you earnestly desire to show hospitality, it is not always easy to know how to proceed. However, I hope that you will struggle with it, rather than simply reconciling yourself to inaction. So, yes, there are risks involved in helping someone stuck on the side of the road. There may indeed be instances where you doubt very much that it would be wise to help. Yet, do not let that stop you from considering each opportunity as it arises.

Here is another example where it is not easy to know how best to show hospitality.

A friend of mine made an 'impulse decision' and ended up pregnant. She and her child needed a place to stay for one week. Personally, I had no objections. We had plenty of room in the house that we were not using. My wife was a bit more hesitant. She feared that one week could turn into two, and two could quickly turn into three. And, we were talking about bringing a young woman into the house. It made my wife uncomfortable and I had to respect that.

In this case, I had to take into account my responsibilities, obligations, love, and respect for my wife, which are all thoroughly biblical. Weighed against my biblically mandated attitudes and duties for my wife, I had to consider my biblically mandated attitudes and duties to my fellow man. I'm not going to let this tension prevent me from never considering it if another opportunity to help someone arises.

I am also aware of the fact that my lack of hospitality, even for 'good' reasons, might impinge on my standing as a leader. Paul understood this. That is why he insisted that a pastor who is not generous to strangers or fellow Christians cannot be an effective leader. Asking his congregation to know the love of Christ and then to not live that same love reduces his credibility significantly.

As a young man, it is easy for your heart to be jaded by various social media images of homeless people and governmental policies. The media has done an exceptional job of creating divisions in our world. These divisions can lead young men to hate others and to act out in violent words or actions.

As a Christian man, you do not have time to well up with anger and bitterness, especially considering that Christ himself gives you unconditional love. An angry, bitter heart is one that does not know the love of Christ. Your relationships now and in the future (for example, in marriage and with your children) depend on your ability to appropriately love those in your home, and those outside.

Lead by example and practice hospitality, even to those who you think are not deserving or worthy—indeed, I have just described everyone, including yourself, who is greatly loved.

What I tell the young ladies:

How does your young man treat strangers? Does he laugh at homeless people? Does he make jokes about homeless people and their plight? If he quips that the person "only wants money for drugs," his heart isn't one that is currently hospitable. If he does not attempt to be helpful even in cases where helping is easy and without risk, that is a clue. Similarly, if you notice that he leaps to help people, even if there might be some danger, you are on the right track.

Chapter 10

Teaching Without a Degree

Now the overseer is to be above reproach, faithful to his wife, temperate, self-controlled, respectable, hospitable, **able to teach**, not given to drunkenness, not violent but gentle, not quarrelsome, not a lover of money.

Able to *Teach*

Greek word: διδακτικoß
Transliterated: didaktikos

Pronounced: did-ak-tik-os'

Being able to teach is definitely an important aspect of a leader in a congregation. The pastor has the responsibility to catechize his congregation. Meaning, he has the responsibility to teach his congregation the truths of Scripture and do it effectively. The Bible is clear about the centrality of the Scriptures[11] for the believer:

> All Scripture is God-breathed and is useful for teaching, rebuking, correcting and training in righteousness, so that the servant of God may be thoroughly equipped for every good work. (2 Timothy 3:16-17)

Thus, it follows that Christians should know the Scriptures so that they can apply them to their faith walk. They need to know the plan of salvation that Christ has set out for them and the rest of mankind. They need to know what salvation looks like manifested in every

[11] The word 'Bible' is often used by Christians to refer to their holy and authoritative writings, but this is a colloquial term more than it is a technical term. It can be thought of as a 'book of books,' but even that doesn't do the matter justice. Included in the Bible are collections of poetry, letters to friends or whole communities, along with sections that read more like 'books.' In light of this diversity, the Jews and early Christians referred to this content not as 'The Bible' but rather 'the Scriptures,' which is to say, simply, 'the Writings.' In this work and the work of many others, the word 'Bible' is used interchangeably with 'the Scriptures.' FYI, 'the Word of God' is also sometimes swapped in. I prefer saying 'the Scriptures.'

breath of life, within every context. Furthermore, the Christian should be able to discern what God's good, pleasing, and perfect will is, so they do not conform to the patterns of this world (Romans 12:1-3). Of course not everyone does this successfully, which makes sense then that Scripture provides guidance and instruction on how to help those that struggle, and singles out certain individuals who have additional responsibility to help their fellow Christians orient their daily lives in light of what the Bible teaches.

That's great if you are going to be pastor, right? Right.

Lest we forget, however, *everyone* is a teacher. Everyone is an influencer. Everyone leads. Just because you are a teenager or a young college male, it does not excuse you from teaching and helping others while walking in the light (1 John 1).

Everyone has friends. Some friends influence positively and some don't. As a young man, it is your responsibility to be able to discern the difference and then be able to restore your friends appropriately as stated in Galatians 6:1, which says:

> Brothers and sisters, if someone is caught in a sin, you who live by the Spirit should restore that person gently. But watch yourselves, or you also may be tempted.

Paul addresses his comment to 'brothers and sisters,' not just the pastor. Paul's admonitions, you see, imply that you, too, should be able to teach effectively. Our behavior, thoughts (manifested), and words influence ourselves and others. In the process of influencing we teach people whether something is acceptable or not. *You already teach in every aspect of your life.* Consider, now, how you can improve your teaching abilities.

Life may be the greatest teacher, but in the classroom, students often need to hear or see information presented differently before being in a position to better learn the concept or idea being presented. There are students that prefer working alone, in partnerships, and in groups. While we often work with partners in my class, we also take time to read and work on our own. We will either create a sketch or mock conversation between an atheist and a Christian. We will lecture but we will also create a timeline on the dry-erase board, so students can see the information simplified. Understanding the different methods of introducing and presenting information is important for teacher, coach, and parent.

Obviously, this book isn't about trendy educational methods

which may or may not be true. My purpose is to draw on three popular learning styles talked about within the field of education to make some points about the different ways we connect with people.

These learning styles are: the kinesthetic learner, the auditory learner, and the visual learner. I will talk about the way we influence people by how we *do* things (kinesthetic) and what we *say and listen* to (auditory). I will combine visual influence with kinesthetic influence because I want to communicate the important fact that *people are influenced by seeing (visual) what you do (kinesthetic).*

As a young man, it is important to remember that everything you say and do impacts and influences other people. Thus, you are teaching people whether you like it or not. You are teaching other people constantly.

Ductus Exemplo: Leadership by example. You cannot escape it. Knowing this brings power to the moment you exist within. Understand that your actions will influence others. Hold your actions up to Scripture and determine whether your action is a positive influence or negative.

Sometimes we teach in the way traditionally understood as 'teaching,' transmitting content in some way. Perhaps it's a play on the basketball court or football practice field. Or, it could be simply how we carry ourselves in our daily lives. Please do not ever think that you are not constantly teaching!

Next, we will explore the three learning styles as spoken about in educational forums, but not from an educational point of view, but rather, from teaching others through influence. That is, we influence (teach) others by what we do and what we say and how we say it. Our lives bleed into the lives of others.[12]

---

[12] **Pro Tip:** For the sake of your own academic and personal growth, I would encourage you to explore the way in which you learn the best. While I *may* have had one or two teachers who assisted me with homework, most teachers just ignored me and passed on by. No one pulled me aside and talked to me about learning or how to better study. I spent a few months being forced to attend a learning center but that was a short-term fix.

I was a poor student that did not pay attention and did not know how to learn. It was not until college that I learned how I best learned. After I made that discovery, my grades improved dramatically. More importantly than the grades, I really began to *learn*.

The more I do something, the more I understand it. I struggle with reading and writing, but if you show me a concept physically, that I can then read

#1: Kinesthetic learners are defined as those who learn by doing activities with their hands, feet, or bodies.

I can watch a basketball game and see an effective move completed, but I will not learn how to do it myself until I do it. I have a friend who can go home and watch videos on Brazilian Jiu-Jitsu moves and gets it immediately. For me, however, in order for me to master the move I have to see it and perform the move repeatedly.

As an older sibling it is very important to understand that your younger siblings are influenced by your actions, *significantly.* My brother had influenced me through his example, and as a result I was able to break some of the negative patterns and dangerous habits I had acquired while growing up. I know firsthand just how important a sibling's leadership is.

Consider this scenario to illustrate what I mean: If you smoke in front of your siblings, they will take that to mean that it is acceptable to smoke. I don't care if you told them, "If you ever do this I will rip the cigarettes out of your mouth and shove it up your nose." If they see you doing it, they will say to themselves, "If it's okay for my big brother, then it must be okay for me too." The damage is done. Likewise, if they never see you smoking then you have influenced them. You may have even opened the door for them to ask you why you do not smoke or if you have ever had pressure to smoke.

Teaching 101: Example. If the teacher is tardy to class, do you really think the student will care about being on time?

The stakes are just as high as a future father and husband. If you slap your wife in the face out of anger, how might your children behave when they are married? If you yell and shout in your arguments, what does that teach them about how to handle differences? Since difficulties are inevitable in a marriage, you had best sort this out quickly!

Of course, we behave this way because we know it is right to do so, but my wife and I also understand that how we interact with each other when there is 'conflict' will send a message. My wife and I do

---

and write afterwards, I will better understand it. If I write my notes out and then type them up, it helps tremendously.

You may wonder why I am spending time on this, but trust me: find a study system or create your own, and orient your studies towards it as much as you can. The sooner you figure it out, the better off you will be educationally. Go find a teacher or parent and have them help you.

not yell at each other. We do not scream. We rarely disagree. When we disagree, we disagree. If there is a need for further discussion, we do so in love.

#2. Auditory: being able to effectively retain information simply by hearing it.

For me, physically meeting expectations would help me better understand them. For others, hearing the expectations would be sufficient. Others could read the same expectations and understand them. In my classroom, I understand this. I know that some students will 'get' something immediately if I present it one way, but that others need it explained differently or in different medium altogether. I go out of my way to accommodate this reality.

Let's consider this again in the context of being a husband and father.

Let me be clear: while it is true that as a husband and father you will definitely have to communicate effectively, it does not mean that you have to take a communications course in college! It does mean that words matter more than you may think.

I see it every day as a father. My children have taken an interest in athletics. I'm not an intellectual. I'm not brilliant, nor am I book smart. Athletics? Athletics I can do. I can play sports. When my children want to learn how to swing a bat, shoot a basketball, or simply play a board game, I have to be able to effectively communicate how to do that.

You cannot yell at your child because they do not swing the bat how you want them to. If you are athletic and you have children, you understand this. There might be different reasons for how you teach one child versus how you teach another. One of your children might enjoy athletics, but might not be a kinesthetic learner. You will have to find a way to teach him or her how to do "x" and it might be different than how you teach your other child, who is an auditory learner. It would be a mistake to assume that just because you learn best in a particular way, your children learn best the same way.

It should go without saying, but... children do not initially know how to accomplish many of the daily activities that we as adults take for granted. They have to be taught! They have to be shown! Things need to be explained! Along with the basic skills of walking, talking, and life in general, you and your spouse will be responsible for teaching them every day how to walk in a manner acceptable to the Lord. Learn how to patiently and clearly communicate your ideas. There are great things at stake.[13]

I see this necessity in the classroom and in athletics every day. Students and players have a lot of great ideas. They want to help others and they want the team to succeed, but they have not learned to communicate effectively because they have not been given a proper example of how to communicate, themselves.

Recently, while at my daughter's basketball game (she was seven at the time), a father was yelling at his daughter because she was not meeting his standards of play. He was loudly criticizing a seven-year-old! He even moved to the bench while she was out to "coach her." What do you think that is going to do for her confidence? How do you think that is going to manifest itself later in life, in competitions and then later, when she is trying to teach her children how to do whatever it is they need to do?

Learn how to communicate effectively.

This leads to the next point: not only do you have to be able to communicate effectively, but never forget that others are seeing how you communicate.

Let me give you another example from my own real life where I have lived out these principles.

For the last fifteen years, I have been playing a World War 2 simulation[14] called "Battleground Europe."

Due to the nature of the simulation, the players you play against are very often the same players you played against before. Well, no one likes to be owned by another player, ever. It is even worse when you are bested by the same dude, over and over. If I do say so myself, I'm pretty good at the simulation, so needless to say, I don't exactly appreciate it when I suffer defeat on the battlefield.

---

[13] **Pro Tip:** As those who know me can attest to, I'm a little competitive. A little too competitive. Because I'm aware of this and I am aware that my actions influence others, I have removed myself from competitive events. Sometimes we have to remove ourselves from certain circumstances for our own spiritual and emotional health, and the health of others. You might be overly competitive, as I am, and might want to consider stepping away from situations that bring out the worst in you. However, the principle can apply to other situations. Are you especially hostile when you lack sleep? Then make it a habit to get good sleep. And so on and so forth.

[14] It is a simulation, not a game! Don't cross me on this!

My command center (my man cave/spare bedroom) is next to the family room where my children read, play games, or watch TV. Being aware that my children are always listening and they do learn by hearing, I have to be very careful with what I say and how I say it.

It is common to hear me say, "Oh, come on," or, "Seriously?" after dying virtually (lag, right?). If you hear a phrase often enough, you tend to make it your own. How many of us can watch a movie and recite the lines shortly after in daily conversations? Imagine hearing the same words over and over. The influence is undeniable. If my children heard me dropping F-bombs every time I died, they would definitely be repeating my words. I know this to be a fact, because my children are often heard saying, "Oh, come on," or, "Seriously?" Seriously.

They echo me every day in word and action. Imagine the conversation with your child's teacher when they explain to you that your child dropped an inappropriate word at school. I would have no one else to blame. Children learn by hearing their parents talk. They learn by hearing their parent's music and television shows. Siblings listen to the conversations you have with your friends, parents, girlfriend, and they take mental notes.

If it is true in relation to how we talk, it is true in relation *to how we live.*

One way or another, parents teach. My parents taught me more by their actions than they did their words. Often it was the message of hard work and contributing positively to whatever activity I was engaged in. Other times, the message was not so beneficial. It was a hard journey to sort out the one from the other in my own life, but now it is my turn to grapple with the reality that as a father, it is me leading positively... or negatively.

I have embraced the challenge, and so should you. You may as well embrace it, because as I have said over and over again, you can't avoid it. Who you are, what you do, and *how you do it* teaches others. You *will* teach your children by your actions, and they in turn, unless the pattern is broken, will teach their children based on the lessons you taught them.

What are you teaching your siblings,
wife and children by your actions every day?

Actions speak louder than words.

Teach wisely.

What I say to the young ladies:

If your young man isn't teaching you the ways of the Lord, he's teaching you the ways of the world. One path will lead you *towards* the cross and the other will take you *away* from the cross. Read Scripture to find out what it looks like to live a sanctified life and ask the young man in your life to teach you appropriately.

Chapter 11

Being Sober Matters

> Now the overseer is to be above reproach, faithful to his wife, temperate, self-controlled, respectable, hospitable, able to teach, **not given to drunkenness**, not violent but gentle, not quarrelsome, not a lover of money.

Not Given to *Drunkenness*

Greek word: παροινος
Transliterated: Paroinos

Pronounced: par'-oy-nos

For the record, I am not a fan of alcohol. More precisely, I hate the impact and influence alcohol has on the world. I hate the world's obsession with it. The idea that you aren't really living unless you drink this or that beer. By itself alcohol is not evil. Humans do an excellent job of making the most of their sinful nature by abusing alcohol.

My personal definition of an alcoholic is one who uses alcohol as a coping mechanism or someone who feels the need to do it without recognizing their need. Merriam-Webster defines alcoholism as, "a medical condition in which someone frequently drinks too much alcohol and becomes unable to live a normal and healthy life." One can argue the definitions and application of the words "normal" and "healthy life."

Many people drink to forget about a problem. It's how they get around or ignore the problem. While we may forget about our problems momentarily, we wake up the next day and the problem is still just as prevalent and relevant as it was the night before.

Many times, alcohol itself becomes the problem. In my experience, a good sign that alcohol itself is the problem is when people begin calling attention to the alcohol use. The usual response to this is to deny, deny, deny. Nobody likes being called out, but if someone lashes out after being called out, the charge is most likely true. When alcohol is the problem, denial can turn deadly and self-destructive.

Our society justifies drinking for any reason. Anytime I've been invited to my (Christian) high school reunion, alcohol was always part of the invitation. Here we are ten, fifteen, and twenty years later and we still need alcohol at the center of our conversations. I am glad that some of my classmates have not followed this pattern. I am glad to see that they have decided on their own to live Christ-centered lives and have concluded that this does not require the assistance of alcohol. Given society's infatuation with alcohol, it goes without saying that my views on the subject don't make me very popular.

Aside from communion on Sunday, the last alcoholic beverage I had was in 2004 or 2005. I was in my man cave playing on the computer. At this time, my wife and I had a roommate who lived in the lower level of our house. He had stepped into the room and I began to converse with him in giggles. I was not drunk but I had lost control of my ability to maintain self-control and be of clear mind. My friend laughed along with me, clearly noticing I had lost full control of my mental capacities.

The next day I reflected on the previous day and I was ashamed. I was the senior theology teacher at the high school I worked at and I was trying to be a godly example for my students and our younger Christian roommate. My actions were not living up to my very own words (let alone Scripture's) and that had to change.

I simply don't want to be around it and I don't want my kids around it either. I know what alcohol does to other people and I know what it does to me if I drink too much. I don't want my kids around a drunken 'me.' Furthermore, I don't want my kids around a culture of alcohol. I grew up in a culture where alcohol was always around. I know personally what kinds of harm it can cause.

Add alcohol to already volatile situations and an explosion is almost inevitable. The irony is that despite its obsession with it, the world is fully aware of the innumerable negative consequences that come from its abuse. Of course, it is not the casual drink that is the concern; it's the accumulation of drinking and the associated attitudes. However, because of the nature of alcohol, it is not at all certain that the drinking will stay 'casual.' I'm not morally opposed to individuals drinking responsibly but I am opposed to the culture of intoxication and the 'you must drink to be one of the guys' culture.

When we serve Christ, our desires of the flesh are crucified along with Christ. Being intoxicated with alcohol (or any other substance, for that matter) does not represent the holiness of God. Ask yourself whether God's holiness would allow himself to overindulge and lose his moral and mental capacities. When you read about Jesus' life, is there anything to suggest to you that Jesus would have ever been found staggering about, punching windows, or performing crazy and often dangerous stunts? Seriously.

As men of the home it is our responsibility to lead our families appropriately. I know many adults who are able to balance a genuine faith with drinking alcohol, but I know many more who are content being overly intoxicated while trying to justify it. It is even worse when the justifications come from Christians and those who are our 'overseers.' I have heard pastors joke about the effects of alcohol Sunday morning while in front of the congregation!

The effects of alcohol and alcohol abuse aren't something to laugh at. 'Liquid courage' isn't courage at all. If you can't be courageous without alcohol, you have bigger issues.

Think alcohol is worth joking about? Read these stats from the Center for Disease Control (CDC):[15]

- In 2014, 9,967 people were killed in alcohol-impaired driving crashes, accounting for nearly one-third (31%) of all traffic-related deaths in the United States.
- Every day, 28 people in the United States die in motor vehicle crashes that involve an alcohol-impaired driver. This amounts to one death every 53 minutes. The annual cost of alcohol-related crashes totals more than $44 billion.
- Excessive alcohol use led to approximately 88,000 deaths and 2.5 million years of potential life lost (YPLL) each year in the United States from 2006 – 2010, shortening the lives of those who died by an average of 30 years.

This isn't a joke. I am sick and tired of the glorification of alcohol. Alcohol destroys families, relationships and futures. We know this, yet we continue to swim in it.

If you watch ESPN, you have seen the many commercials with attractive women standing next to men drinking alcohol. These commercials scream: "The party life, that's where it is at." Sadly, most young men are engrossed in the culture of professional sports and the culture of alcohol and will easily resonate with such messaging. What seems innocuous and fun is actually very harmful.

Objections to my position will abound, so let's address two of

[15] http://www.cdc.gov/alcohol/fact-sheets/alcohol-use.htm

them.

It will be said: "Drinking alcohol itself is not a sin, and moreover, underage drinking and getting drunk do not have anything to do with God's holiness."

Let's settle the underage drinking aspect of the argument quickly:

> Let everyone be subject to the governing authorities, for there is no authority except that which God has established. The authorities that exist have been established by God. Consequently, whoever rebels against the authority is rebelling against what God has instituted, and those who do so will bring judgment on themselves... (Romans 13:1-2)

If you are a resident of the United States, the drinking age is twenty-one. Underage drinking violates the law and thus violates Scripture. It does not matter if your parents supply or not.[16] Hosting tent parties and underage drinking is not legal. Allowing our underage children to party while we supervise is neither biblical nor prudent. Individuals who try to justify underage drinking choose to ignore Scripture. If we are talking about being a godly man, choosing to ignore Scripture is not wise.

What about *legal* drinking? As a young man who is twenty-one or older, you are obviously allowed to drink legally. Have your drink—but if you do not show restraint and if alcohol is the culture of your family, do not be surprised if your children end up with DUI's (like I almost did), poor test grades, poor athletic performance, sexual promiscuity, physical injury or worse: death.

Scripture is clear, while you have the freedom to drink legally, the line stops at getting drunk,

> The acts of the flesh are obvious: sexual immorality, impurity and debauchery; idolatry and witchcraft; hatred, discord, jealousy, fits of rage, selfish ambition, dissensions, factions and envy; drunkenness, orgies, and the like. I warn you, as I did before, that those who

[16] Granted, there are states like Wisconsin, which allow for underage drinking in specific circumstances. For example, there must be close parental supervision; and it must be your own parent. Nonetheless, the majority of states don't allow it, except with the very narrow exception of religious ceremonies like having wine for communion.

> live like this will not inherit the kingdom of God. (Galatians 5:19-21)

Every year we hear of examples of students who have died because they were involved in the alcohol culture. Too many students believe that it will never happen to them.

I cannot recall the number of poor decisions I made while intoxicated. I do, however, remember my almost DUI. My parents were having a little get-together. They had left some of their alcohol on the front the porch. I was heading out to a friend's house and grabbed three beers. I hid them in my car and started to drink them once I arrived. After a couple of beers my friend and I had a little fight. He kicked me out of the house. To get home, I 'only' had to drive a little over one mile. As luck would have it, a cop coming from the other direction turned around and followed me. To say I was nervous would be an understatement. I knew that if he pulled me over, I would get a DUI. For this one-time bad decision, the entire trajectory of my life could have been altered, and not in a good way.

Had I not gone off to college, I am very certain that my underage drinking and alcohol abuse would have continued and the results would not have been pleasant. I know this because I have seen it happen in the lives of so many other people.

Don't think you are off the hook, just because you are merely 'buzzed.' Drinking to a buzz is too far because your body is still being influenced by the alcohol. You are close to being drunk and thus closer to making bad decisions.

Listen. *You do not have to drink when you go to college. If you are in college already, it is perfectly fine to stop drinking.* It's also perfectly fine to contemplate how serious you take your faith. The pressure and presence of alcohol is significant in college and as an adult. Consider the long lasting impact your drinking will have, not only on your marriage but your children.

The numbers regarding alcohol consumption is ridiculous. Here are stats regarding binge drinking from the Center for Disease Control (CDC). The CDC defines 'binge drinking' as,

> a pattern of drinking that brings a person's blood alcohol concentration (BAC) to 0.08 grams percent or above. This typically happens when men consume 5 or more drinks, and when women consume 4 or more

drinks, in about 2 hours.[17]

One in six U.S. adults binge drinks about four times a month, consuming about eight drinks per binge. More information from the CDC website:

- While binge drinking is more common among young adults aged 18–34 years, binge drinkers aged 65 years and older report binge drinking more often—an average of five to six times a month.
- Approximately 92% of U.S. adults who drink excessively report binge drinking in the past 30 days.
- Although college students commonly binge drink, 70% of binge drinking episodes involve adults age 26 years and older.
- The prevalence of binge drinking among men is twice the prevalence among women.
- Binge drinkers are 14 times more likely to report alcohol-impaired driving than non-binge drinkers.
- About 90% of the alcohol consumed by youth under the age of 21 in the United States is in the form of binge drinks.
- More than half of the alcohol consumed by adults in the United States is in the form of binge drinks.

Binge drinking is associated with many health problems, including:

- Unintentional injuries (e.g., car crashes, falls, burns, drowning)
- Intentional injuries (e.g., firearm injuries, sexual assault, domestic violence)
- Alcohol poisoning
- Sexually transmitted diseases
- Unintended pregnancy
- Children born with Fetal Alcohol Spectrum Disorders
- Liver disease
- Neurological damage

It's obvious to those around alcohol that it has a dark side that you want to avoid. So what can you do? Draw your line. Don't cross

[17] http://www.cdc.gov/alcohol/fact-sheets/binge-drinking.htm

it. It sounds very simple and it really is. Don't drink. Don't go to the party. Remove yourself from any situation that has alcohol. No one forces you into a car to go to a party. You choose to get in the car. You choose to stay. Walk home. Go somewhere else. Removing yourself may seem judgmental, but people will get over it. *You do not have to drink alcohol if you do not want to drink alcohol.*

Scripture is clear: avoid the deeds of darkness. This position does not make me Mr. Popular with many people, but I'm not interested in a popularity contest. I have seen what it does to people's decisions and attitudes. Most likely, you have, too. If enough of us come around to the facts concerning alcohol, maybe it would be the drinkers who are unpopular, instead of the other way around!

There was a line drawn in the sand a long time ago that I decided I was not going to cross. It didn't matter to me who was doing or saying what, I wasn't going to cross it myself.[18] It can be hard to maintain your convictions when there is so much pressure to do the opposite, but if you are determined to start at the cross, it's actually quite easy. Galatians 1:10 has been a powerful reminder to me to draw 'lines,' and also encouragement to not cross them:

> Am I now trying to win the approval of human beings, or of God? Or am I trying to please people? If I were still trying to please people, I would not be a servant of Christ.

It ultimately has to come down to who am I serving and who am I trying to please. Paul's words speak to the assurance that the Gospel he received is the same Gospel he is passing onto the others. This wasn't making him many friends. He was flogged, stoned, and jailed. Paul had drawn his line in the sand and he was not going to give in simply because people didn't like him or the message. He wasn't trying to please men, he was trying to preach the Gospel and serve Christ.

---

[18] As a teacher of high school seniors I am often invited to graduation parties. There is often drinking and sometimes the recently graduated senior is drinking, too! On such occasions I will remind the student what I had said often in class, and politely excuse myself. I don't have to participate in activities I don't approve of, and neither do you. If others insist on participating in dangerous (and often, illegal) activities, in love and with their interests in mind, you may want to call attention to what is going on, but don't be afraid to leave.

Draw your line and don't cross it.

If you cross it, don't you dare try to pressure others into crossing it in order to make yourself feel better about your decisions. If you do that, you are no man at all.

I have been speaking with high school and college students in mind, but we should remember that eventually you'll likely have kids. If you've courageously stood your ground, you'll want to equip them to stand theirs, too.

Life tends to provide ample opportunities to instruct children. Due to the widespread acceptance of alcohol use and abuse, you can bet you'll have plenty of opportunities to teach them about the nature of alcohol and how it relates to a godly lifestyle. Don't be afraid to seize these opportunities. It is far better to talk openly about the subject early and often, then to ignore it. If you don't give them instruction and guidance, you can be sure they'll get it from their peers and society in general.

Also, if they are asking questions, don't be disturbed by this fact. Questions are learning opportunities.

Bottom line: your *example*, what you do and how you do it, will directly influence your children and their children. How you parent will influence how your children will be as parents. My wife and I made a decision that we didn't want to follow the world's lead on the subject of alcohol (or anything else, for that matter). We wanted a different pattern for our children.

What pattern will you create?

What I say to the young ladies:

One of the reasons I like the United States Marine Corps so much is because they talk about courage—not only physical courage, but moral courage. As a coach and teacher, I want athletes and students who have *moral courage*. I want to grow individuals who will stand up for the truth regardless of the cost. If your young man is taking you to parties to drink and become intoxicated, he's leading you the wrong way. If he knows it is wrong, he lacks the moral courage to do what is right. You should think hard about whether or not you want someone like this in your life. If he lacks the moral courage when it comes to something like alcohol abuse, are you so sure he'll have it when it comes to being faithful to you?

Chapter 12

You Don't Have to Argue

Now the overseer is to be above reproach, faithful to his wife, temperate, self-controlled, respectable, hospitable, able to teach, not given to drunkenness**, not violent but gentle, not quarrelsome**, not a lover of money.

Not violent but gentle, not quarrelsome

Greek word: επιεικες and πλεκτες
Transliterated: Epieikes and Plektes

Pronounced: ep-ee-i-kace and plake'-tace

According to Strong's Concordance, "epieikes" means "gentle." The word used along with "epieikes" is "plektes," which means, "not a striker." Thus, Paul is telling us that an overseer is to be one who is gentle and not one who strikes or is a brawler.

Any adult can tell you, life happens. On average we work forty to fifty hours a week. Jobs can be stressful. Finances can be tight. Relationships can be stressful. Being a parent can be stressful. Little Johnny likes to mouth off and push the limits. Unfortunately, many people do not deal with their stress effectively. Many turn to the bottle. Some lose control of themselves in other ways. And then...

Out of the blue, for the first time ever, Little Johnny receives a smack across the face.

I'm not necessarily opposed to physical punishment. I am opposed to a parent losing control and reacting out of anger. The many pressures of life can build up inside someone and then vent in ways that even the individual losing control are surprised by. Unloading on the people we love is an obvious context for venting, because those people tend to be in closer proximity than everyone else. One might expect, then, that these outbursts become something we regret, perhaps for our entire lives.

It is possible to do something that there is no coming back from.

After a long day of work, you really have to be on your A-game because your children will make mistakes that you will have to respond to. How you respond has life-changing influence on your children. It takes mental discipline and patience to maintain control while you are under strain.

If your own parents were ones to lash out when stressed, the chances are that you will behave that way, too. You will have learned by imitation. Unless you break the cycle, how you were parented is how you will parent, which in turn influences how your children will parent. Similarly, if your father pushed your mother around, you will gravitate towards the same behaviors. If your own child sees this, he too will likely imitate the abuse.

If this at all describes you, then it is up to you to do what you need to do to break the pattern.

Note, in this I am not at all assuming that there was not love in these relationships. In fact, the odds are very good that everyone involved deeply regretted what transpired. They wish that they could go back and do it over, and this time do it right. I am trying to spare you of this. Instead of wishing you have a 'do over' realize that your moment of choice is almost upon you and prepare yourself to conduct yourself appropriately the first time.

Learning self-control will pay dividends throughout your life in various contexts. While it is easier to lose control on the ones nearest you, our society is littered with the fall out of people losing control in a variety of settings. You do not want to add to that fall out!

When I was in college I had a bad attitude when I played athletics. One time, during church basketball, I was getting hacked up pretty bad and I was frustrated with the referee, who clearly did not care about my physical well-being. He and I had had other run-ins before this game, but this was the tipping point. Running down the court next to him I said, "Someone is going to get hurt." In which the referee replied, "Hopefully it's you." I found that to be absurd.

Later in the game, he called a foul in my favor and I was shooting free throws. I had made the first one, but he called it back saying I had crossed the free throw line. I had not. I backed up a bit, not much, and made my next free throw. Citing another lane violation, he called that one back too. I had enough. I quit. I walked off the court. Actually, I went and sat in the bleachers with the rest of the spectators. I think I am also the only person to ever receive a technical foul while being a spectator: at one point I 'sarcastically' clapped, and the referee hit me with the penalty.

The reader probably is reading that and thinking that, given the referee's behavior, my own behavior was understandable and justified. However, 'understandable' and 'justifiable' is not the same as 'appropriate' and 'honorable.' I can't control another person's conduct, but I can control my own. In this instance, I made a choice in anger and frustration that amounted to one, simple, disgraceful thing: I had abandoned my team. That alone was enough for anyone in the stands to see my character and my ability to deal with hardship. How would I behave if something happened in life and quitting wasn't an option? Probably, I would do what tends to happen in such scenarios; I'd bottle it up and vent it out on those close to me.

Indeed, my lack of self-control when it came to athletics would continue to manifest. My behavior toward some opponents and referees was inexcusable. I was not responsible for instigating conflict, but I certainly took advantage of the opportunity to let the referee know that their call was terrible. If an opponent opened his mouth, I responded, tit for tat. While I did not cuss anyone out or flip anyone off, my actions and voice were equivalent. Actions speak louder than words, and my actions were screaming arrogance, immaturity, and a lack of gentleness and self-control.

I did not like where my head was at while playing competitive sports. My senior year of college, I withdrew from playing intramural sports. It was that bad.

If you aren't under stress, controlling yourself is a piece of cake. It is no credit to your self-control if you are even-handed when everything is going great. It is only when the pressure is on that you have a chance to exercise your self-control. That said, if you don't think you can keep yourself under control, even if it is not a 'credit' to you, per se, it is generally better to take yourself out of that situation than stay in it and do something you might regret.[19]

As a coach, if I have players who cannot control themselves physically or verbally on the field, they have a warm spot on the

---

[19] My brother tells me that he went years being irritable with his family in the morning and then in the evening as bedtime approached. He did not understand why relatively minor inconveniences would rile him up so much. Eventually it dawned on him that his habit of staying up late and getting up early for work was taking a toll. He just could not be the kind of person he wanted to be while sleep-deprived. He changed his sleep habits and his relationship with his wife and children improved immediately for the simple reason that his own behavior improved. To put it differently, in order to exert self-control, he knew he needed to change his circumstances. He couldn't avoid being irritable when tired, but he *could* avoid being tired.

bench until they calm down. What we do and *how* we do what we do influences who we will be later on in life. As a Christian man, it's important to understand priorities and perspective. Participating in athletics does not place Christian character on hold. If you cannot control yourself and are taking your athletics too seriously, it may be prudent to step away from them. An easy way to avoid having to do that is to remember that kicking a ball into the back of a net, or shooting an orange ball in an orange rim isn't that important in the larger scheme of life. Prioritize and gain perspective on what matters and play to the glory of that perspective.

This is probably a good point to segue into discussing the avoidance of being quarrelsome. The Greek word is "amacos," which means "peaceable" and to "abstain from fighting."

I have provided unfortunately good examples of what a quarrelsome individual looks like—me, in some of my most shameful moments.

We all know individuals who are more interested in fighting than they are growing. In the classroom I make it very clear that I am not interested in arguing with the students. I am interested in growing and learning. In so many words, I tell the students, "If you are only interested in arguing for the sake of arguing, save it. I'm not interested. I am not going to waste the emotional and spiritual energy entertaining your desire to cause distraction or dissension. Do not ask questions if you really have no interest in the answer."

Believe it or not, I have had students disappointed because we do not scream at each other in the classroom. There are some students who become frustrated with me because they will ask a question and are ignored. I had a student once tell me, "I really thought we would be arguing more about "x." Dude. I don't care about "x." It has no relation to anything we are talking about in class. If you want to argue, go argue in the mirror. This sets the tone early on that the focus of the class is learning and growing. If you as a young man are more interested in hearing your own voice than you are learning, I would recommend not talking at all.

Proverbs 26:4 reads, "Do not answer a fool according to his folly, or you yourself will be just like him." Arguing for the sake of arguing prevents growth. Instead, listen. It takes discipline and patience to not entertain pointless arguments, but it is possible. It helps a great deal if you are not the one who initiates them in the first place!

There are plenty of other times in life when you will need to control yourself when you are under stress. Your job might not be going great, priming you to explode on your boss or perhaps be snippy with customers. You might be having a bad day and find yourself pulled over by a police officer, who has no idea that you are already on edge. You might even be that police officer, and it is *you* who is on edge. Your lack of self-control, quarrelsome habits, and inclination towards violent outbursts will have many opportunities to manifest, unless you master them.

When you are fighting to protect your image or using your emotion to argue, it's not going to go well. If you are overly prideful, then it will be difficult to have a healthy relationship with your spouse. I know this from personal experience. Thankfully, the large stick protruding from my eye has been removed and I am less prideful and quarrelsome than I was before. When you realize it's more about him and less about you, your perspective changes.

When talking about coping with stress in a healthy way, it is important to understand that people experience stress in different ways. However, they are not all so different that we cannot recognize commonalities, varying according to 'personality type.' I highly recommend taking a legitimate personality test. Such a test will help you understand the kind of person you are, how you generally operate, and the kinds of things you will be inclined to do when in conflict.

I took Florence Littauer's *Personality Plus* test. I'm more of a Powerful Choleric and my wife is more of the Peaceful Phlegmatic type. You do not know what those are yet, but you are smart enough to put the first words of each next to each other:

Powerful vs. Peaceful.

Which one do you think would be more argumentative than the other? My wife knows this. I know this. Despite that, we do not argue much. We have never yelled, screamed, or cussed each other out. "Never?" you ask. Never. There are multiple reasons for that, one of them being that my wife is so peaceful and quiet. By her nature, not only does she not enjoy conflict, she also does not waste time engaging in pointless arguments. In short, she is primed to ignore my outbursts. I am not sure how she has remained so patient over the years, but she wins. I can only imagine the conversations she has in her own head about me when I am talking with her!

It is worth pointing out, though, that one of the other reasons we don't argue much is because we don't have much to argue and fight about. Remember my counsel about removing yourself from a situation where you don't think you'll be able to control yourself? It works the other way, too. You can put yourself into a situation where you will be better able to control yourself. Wisely choosing a partner for a life time commitment such as marriage will go a long way towards softening your edges.

In our case, my wife and I share a common starting point for all of our conversations and decisions: The Cross. Scripture, while primarily given to us to show us our need for a savior in Christ, also shows us what living as a redeemed child of God looks like. Christ has made us a new creation and He has grown that new life within us. All of our conversations are based from that salvation and sanctification. Discussions on makeup, haircuts, what clothes to wear, where to spend money, how fast to drive (or not drive) is all based off of the same worldview.

This shared worldview has generated some other helpful attributes. For example, we are both parochial school teachers. We are used to not having much money. Given the fact that she's much better at balancing the books, and there isn't much money to begin with, when she tells me when and if we have money to spend, I just go along with it. Other areas of possible friction are smoothed out in a similar fashion and for similar reasons. Choosing a compatible mate turns out to be a wonderful way to control the worst parts of your nature.

Hopefully the reader can see the corollary to that: Choosing an incompatible mate might be a recipe for disaster! Choose wisely.

There will be plenty of people out there that will say that if you are not arguing and having a good scream with your girlfriend (and spouse) you do not have a healthy relationship. I take issue with that. If your relationship is marked by a lot of yelling and screaming, that might be a sign that there are serious incompatibilities in the relationship. However, just like you do not have to drink alcohol, you also do not have to yell and scream. You do not have to argue. There are multiple verses that influence this conclusion.

Let's remember that the main point of the Scriptures is to show us our need for a savior. A core message of the Scriptures is that we are all in the same boat: we are all sinners and we are all in need of a savior. Therefore, no one can boast they are more spiritual or morally superior than someone else. Nonetheless, in some respects, the Scriptures are very clear about how we are to conduct ourselves within our relationships:

> Be completely humble and gentle; be patient, bearing with one another in love. Make every effort to keep the unity of the Spirit through the bond of peace. There is one body and one Spirit, just as you were called to one hope when you were called; one Lord, one faith, one baptism; one God and Father of all, who is over all and through all and in all. (Ephesians 4:2)

> Therefore, as God's chosen people, holy and dearly loved, clothe yourselves with compassion, kindness, humility, gentleness and patience. Bear with each other and forgive one another if any of you has a grievance against someone. Forgive as the Lord forgave you. (Colossians 3:12-13)

What part of those verses in their context can you argue against? I don't get the impression that 'yelling and screaming' is part and parcel of a healthy, godly, relationship, do you? To the contrary: Be completely humble and gentle. Be patient. Clothe yourself with the same compassion, kindness, and humility Christ has given you. Arguing for the sake of arguing is being immature, arrogant, and self-centered.

Rarely do I have to use this next verse in response to an argumentative student, but it has happened. It is Romans 12:3:

> For by the grace given me I say to every one of you: Do not think of yourself more highly than you ought, but rather think of yourself with sober judgment, in accordance with the faith God has distributed to each of you.

Part of the larger context is that Paul is speaking to the body of Christ and the various roles and responsibilities within the body. Romans 12:3 is a good reminder to not think of yourself more highly than you ought (Philippians 2:3), but keep in mind how sinful you are and how much in need of a savior *you are.* You are in need of just as much grace as the next person. When everyone proceeds from this basis, it is much easier—and healthier—for everyone.

Where does this leave you? I don't know. Maybe you have cussed me out already and said to yourself, "He has no idea who I am?" or "He has no idea what I have had to deal with in my life." Tell yourself what you must, but being angry and bitter is not going to solve anything. If we take this anger and bitterness and habit of being quarrelsome into relationships, it will hinder growth.

In the Christian church, Paul recognized this. It is one of the reasons why Paul said an overseer should be gentle and not quarrelsome. Imagine a pastor who simply argues with his parishioners and never actually listens, doing what he wants, when he wants. The Christian church will not grow and neither will those entrusted to his care. Private conversations with a quarrelsome pastor will not end well.

Yet, Paul's admonitions apply to all of us, not just pastors. Humility goes a long way in relationships. Our choice is to embrace the humility and sacrifice Christ has given us and extend it to others, or continue to be prideful and full of bitterness and arrogance.

What you do, and how you do it, influences who you will be in the future. It will also influence how you are as a spouse and as a parent. It will influence your children, and through them, your grand-children.

What do you do and how will you do
what you have been called to do?

What I say to the young ladies:

It is easy to tell whether or not your boyfriend is more interested in exercising power rather than being peaceful. Is he controlling? Is he telling you who you can hang out with? Reading your text messages? The amount of drama involved in young relationships is not only embarrassing, it's unnecessary. Consider the arguments you find yourself in with your boyfriend. Do they have anything to do with anything that is worth arguing about? If he's more interested in arguing for the sake of arguing, prepare for a stressful and emotionally draining relationship. You want someone who will build you up, not tear you down. Move on while you can. Better yet, don't put yourself in that situation in the first place. Seek out godly young men who behave with maturity. Bear in mind, though, that even a mature young man might have a personality type that doesn't mesh well with your own. When you are seeking a mate, use your head, not just your heart.

Chapter 13

Rich in Christ

> Now the overseer is to be above reproach, faithful to his wife, temperate, self-controlled, respectable, hospitable, able to teach, not given to drunkenness, not violent but gentle, not quarrelsome, **not a lover of money**.

Not a lover of money

Greek Word: αφιλαργυρος
Transliterated: Aphilarguros

Pronounced: af-il-ar'-goo-ros

Do not covet and do not be greedy.

We learn these basic tenants in the Ten Commandments. We learn to not covet our neighbor's house, wife or possessions. Instead, we are told to be content with the providence of God. A greedy heart is focused on the desires of the flesh. "Give me more!" A heart that covets ignores the blessings that God has already provided. "Give me what they have, God!" God responds with a lesson of the sparrows:

> Therefore, I tell you, do not worry about your life, what you will eat or drink; or about your body, what you will wear. Is not life more than food, and the body more than clothes? Look at the birds of the air; they do not sow or reap or store away in barns, and yet your heavenly Father feeds them. Are you not much more valuable than they? Can any one of you by worrying add a single hour to your life?
>
> And why do you worry about clothes? See how the flowers of the field grow. They do not labor or spin. Yet I tell you that not even Solomon in all his splendor was dressed like one of these. If that is how God clothes the grass of the field, which is here today and tomorrow is thrown into the fire, will he not much more clothe you—you of little faith? (Matthew 6:25-30)

A consistent message, demonstrated in both the Old Testament and the New Testament, is that God provides for His people. That is ironic, because the Scriptures also record that His people continually want God to give them more. I can only imagine God saying to himself, "What else do you want? I have delivered you from slavery, I have provided you manna in the desert, I have opened a body of water to save you. I have given you freedom from the law by providing you The Christ. And you want more? More of what you do not need?"

Their answer, and ours is, "Yes! Give me more."

Being content is very difficult. As I already mentioned, there was a time in my life when I lacked contentment and purpose. Seeking to create my own purpose, I blotted out God's design and purpose for me. His purpose for me was not fame and fortune, but rather leading young men and women. I am satisfied with this purpose, and this satisfaction has brought its own rewards.

Paul is right to advise Timothy that an overseer is one that should not be a lover of money. A lover of money is not a lover of God because the heart's attention is misplaced. Paul makes special note of this later in 1 Timothy 6:

> For we brought nothing into the world, and we can take nothing out of it. But if we have food and clothing, we will be content with that. Those who want to get rich fall into temptation and a trap and into many foolish and harmful desires that plunge people into ruin and destruction. For the love of money[20] is a root of all kinds of evil. Some people, eager for money, have wandered from the faith and pierced themselves with many griefs.

Isn't that the truth? Those who love money often find themselves in greater trouble than where they were originally. Just as contentment brings its own rewards, fame and fortune bring their

---

[20] This passage is often quoted incorrectly. You will hear people say, "Money is the root of all evil." But that is not what it says. It specifically says that it is the *love* of money that is the issue, and by saying it is *a* root, not *the* root, the passage leaves it wide open for evil to come about for other reasons. Thus it follows from the passage that money itself is not *necessarily* the problem and that it is actually possible to not love money and yet still carry out evil. Conversely, it does not follow from this passage that 'money' is intrinsically evil. Clearly, however, dangers surround it on all sides.

own pitfalls.

An Internet search will provide you with many examples of individuals who became rich only to become poor both monetarily as well as spiritually. Instead of being content with who they are in Christ, many individuals want to become famous only because they want lots of people to know who they are. Here is a truth: when we start at the cross, we are *already* famous, because of the greatness of Christ. What else do you need? Christ, the maker and redeemer of the universe, *knows* you. Isn't that more than enough?

Money cannot buy him, and more money cannot get you more of him. You have all of him through faith. Given this relationship, you can well understand why Paul is astonished that people could still lack contentment. You are rich beyond belief because you were bought not with money or possessions, but with the blood of God himself (1 Corinthian 6:9-10).

We can be filthy rich and at the same time be spiritually bankrupt. We can be filthy poor but spiritually rich. This is a point that Paul makes often. For example, in Philippians 3 he provides a list of boasts he could make about himself:

> If someone else thinks they have reasons to put confidence in the flesh, I have more: circumcised on the eighth day, of the people of Israel, of the tribe of Benjamin, a Hebrew of Hebrews; in regard to the law, a Pharisee; as for zeal, persecuting the church; as for righteousness based on the law, faultless. But whatever were gains to me I now consider loss for the sake of Christ. What is more, I consider everything a loss because of the surpassing worth of knowing Christ Jesus my Lord, for whose sake I have lost all things. I consider them garbage, that I may gain Christ and be found in him, not having a righteousness of my own that comes from the law, but that which is through faith in Christ—the righteousness that comes from God on the basis of faith.

Translation: Paul was the man. Or, so he thought he was at one time. He had everything *but* Christ. He literally calls his status and greatness "skubalon," or excrement![21]

Money is not intrinsically evil or sinful, but it certainly is connected to many kinds of evil. Yes, it is important to be in a position to provide for your family and the future of your family. However, it is more important to provide spiritually for your family.

We are certainly blessed to live in America where we have freedom and opportunities that many people do not have. Along with that freedom and those opportunities are temptations to pursue roads to things that are not spiritually healthy. Given our country's great wealth, I suppose it is probably true for everyone, but I am constantly having to put myself in place, making sure I am content with God's provision for me. This can sometimes be a struggle.

Paul is reminding Timothy that an overseer is one whose starting point is always the cross. If the overseer does not start at the cross, then the overseer is misleading God's people. It is no different for a husband or a young man. If he is more interested in the hottest car or gadget than he is providing for his family spiritually, he is missing the point. If the family is building up material possessions but does not have Christ, they are empty.

It is easy for high school young men to be distracted by the illusion of worldly success. According to the world, you have arrived if you have a fast car, loads of money, and a trophy wife. Music, television, movies, and printed material all support this idea of success.

Which one sounds more appealing to the majority of high school boys: Being rich in Christ or owning the latest V8 Camaro? Having a girlfriend who is grounded in Christ or one who is the hottest in the school?

Our society encourages us to want the best and to covet and lust after what we cannot have. Scripture encourages us to seek after Christ. The Camaro will eventually wither away into oblivion. Christ will last an eternity. The girl may be super attractive, but is she leading you towards the cross? Are you leading *her* to the cross? One direction leads you to knowledge and understanding of God's grace. One does not. Choose wisely.

---

[21] The NIV translates "skubalon" as "garbage," which does not do Paul's language justice. In fact, even calling it 'excrement' doesn't do it justice. There is a certain four-letter word that is probably the most accurate translation of "skubalon." I bet you can guess which one it is.

The early Christian church existed differently than today. They worshipped in homes, often under the threat of persecution. All they wanted was each other and to be with Christ. If they didn't have anything else, they didn't care. A practice of the early Christian church was to pool their resources together and help one another out:

> They sold property and possessions to give to anyone who had need. Every day they continued to meet together in the temple courts. They broke bread in their homes and ate together with glad and sincere hearts, praising God and enjoying the favor of all the people. And the Lord added to their number daily those who were being saved. (Acts 2:45-47)

The converts to Christianity were rich and poor, Jew and Gentile. Pooling their resources together could have made it tempting for an overseer to take advantage of his congregational resources for his own benefit. That is a story that has played out over the centuries in full view of the public. One does not have to look far to find taking advantage of their position of leadership to enrich themselves, rather than their brothers and sisters. This brings shame on Christ and his Church.

But we will say it again: Paul's admonitions do not only apply to the overseer. Wealth and wanting more distracts us from caring for those who need. That's why it is important that you as a young man come to a conclusion as to whom you will serve, the world or the Word. One of those options carries a more significant consequence than the other.

I get it. It is a struggle, and one that I have to endure more often than I'd like. It's tempting to want and to want more. It's that more does mean anything, let alone without Christ. Remember what Paul said. It is all excrement.

Recently, a young woman whom I had the pleasure of teaching invited me to lunch to talk about the ministry work she was doing on a college campus. At the end of the lunch she asked me if I would be willing to contribute monthly to her cause. The money would be going towards a worthy effort, the ministry of Christ. I gave her my word that I could contribute. A couple months had passed. I had full intention of contributing but I became side tracked by selling our house. I was allocating our funds towards the house and ignored my word to help a sister. It took me almost a year to follow through with my verbal commitment. Finally, I went to donate but learned that the woman was no longer working at the university. She had packed up and gone home. I was so focused on the material gain of the house that I failed to focus on her ministry of sharing the Word. I failed. The apology that I sent via social media was read but unanswered. I don't blame her.

I wanted a better looking house and sacrificed a friendship as well as opportunities for her to share the Gospel. I remind students of 1 Timothy 6:10, which says, "Some people, eager for money, have wandered from the faith and pierced themselves with many griefs." Why are we so concerned with material possessions? It's a phone. It's not your lifeline. It's not your friend. It's a phone. It is a car, not your spouse. It is a thing, not a person. Things will fade away. Persons will be raised from the dead and live forever, either with Christ... or without him. Keep it in perspective.

Failing to do so means we are more apt to wander from the faith, and in doing so probably create even more problems for themselves. The consequences of wandering from His grace are at times blatantly obvious and at other times subtle. While we think we are in a good place spiritually, we may be far from the cross and not even know it. We must constantly be on our guard.

A godly man is one who stays rooted at the cross. The world is full of examples of failing at manhood. This is precisely why Christ came into the world to save mankind from their failures. He succeeded in every way we cannot.

In the Old Testament, the priest was the man who went before God on behalf of the people. In the New Testament, Christ becomes The High Priest, the manliest man of all men who have ever existed, more manly than all men, combined. This man chose not worldly riches, but to sacrifice himself for us. Through him, we have direct access to the grace of God. We should be imitating him, the World.

May our hearts and minds always be focused on growing in the knowledge of Christ, so that we may lead others towards the cross, where they, too, will meet Christ.

If we are not starting at the cross, we are starting somewhere else! Are we more interested in growing our social or monetary banks, or growing in the grace and knowledge of Christ?

What I say to the young ladies:

If he's trying to buy your affection, he clearly has a misplaced heart. What kind of car he has may impress his friends, but if his slick car and fancy clothing are at the center of his existence then that means the center of his existence is not on God. If his focus is not on God but on his cars and money, and he's your boyfriend, then which way do you think he's going to be leading you? In that same spirit, if you are more impressed by his car than the one driving it, you also have a misplaced heart. It's time to look at your priorities, and put things in perspective. What is more important? Things that wither away and rot or that which will live forever?

PART III

Chapter 14

So Now What?

That's a fair question. Reading the book could leave you discouraged. Let me share with you a few reminders:

1) Ultimately, this is about Christ. In all things we start at the cross. At the cross we see our sin, salvation, and His work of sanctification through you. Whatever you do, you do it to the glory of God.

2) One of the most important encouragements you can get from this book is that *you have a choice.* The decisions you make are in your control. While it is true that you will have inherited many attitudes and behaviors from your family, you have a powerful ally helping you: God himself. He has promised to give us his Holy Spirit. With the Holy Spirit empowering us, we should not doubt our ability to make changes. The habits you have now are ones that you yourself made. If you made them, you can un-make them, and make new ones, with the power of God at your back.

3) With this in mind, we start our habits at the cross, recognizing that we are sinful and despite all of our best efforts, we will fall short. If we didn't fall short, we would not need Christ. But, not only do we need Christ, we *have* Christ. No, Christ *has* us!

I would like to address an attitude that I sometimes encounter. On the one hand, there are people who, like King David said in Psalm 51, have their "sin always before them." That is, they are so acutely aware of their sin that they can't bring themselves to accept the forgiveness that has been offered to them. On the other hand, though, are those who think their sins are 'no big deal.' They think they are relatively small things. Worse, perhaps, they dismiss their faults because 'they meant well.' As if merely having good intentions outweighed negative consequences!

Carefully read 1 John 1:8-9:

> If we claim to be without sin, we deceive ourselves and the truth is not in us. If we confess our sins, he is faithful and just and will forgive us our sins and purify us from all unrighteousness.

There is a sense in which we can take our sin too seriously—that is, even more seriously than God himself takes it... and He takes it very seriously! That is not healthy. But it is also not healthy if you don't take it seriously enough. There is danger at the extremes. You want to go right down the middle. Acknowledge your sin, accept that we will fall short, but take comfort in the fact that in Christ we are forgiven. We are free to live, putting our confidence in Christ, rather than ourselves.

A good way of putting our confidence in Christ is to ground our lives in the Scriptures, which testify about Christ.

Part of the confusion for young men and women is that all too often we read the world into the Word as opposed to the Word into the world. What we want to be true from a worldly point of view isn't true from a Scriptural point of view. We twist ourselves into pretzels to justify our behaviors or desires. Worse yet, many men and women who are in positions of great influence lead young men and women from a worldly point of view as opposed to starting with the Word.

Every year, I tell my students that commenting on the Bible without actually having read it, is intellectually dishonest. When we know what the Bible says, and attempt to ground our lives on it, many things take care of themselves. When we meditate on the Word of God day and night (Joshua 1:8), we place ourselves in a position for the Spirit to work through us. This allows us to focus on starting at the cross rather than conforming to the patterns of this world (Romans 12:2).

So, don't be discouraged. God has given us his Spirit and he has given us his Word. If you become discouraged, open up the Bible and study it. Put your faith in God's promises rather than your own efforts. Trust God, not your feelings about God. In that vein...

4) Take a stand on God's Word. Trust that the one who made you and the entire universe knows what He is doing! Get your advice about how to be a man of God from God, not the world! In other words, decide that you want to be a man of God.

There is a temptation after listening to the numerous stories of my epic failures for you to conclude, "Well, he turned out okay." By the Grace of God! Another may conclude the opposite, "Well, he is a guy who tries, and even he fails, so what chance do I have?" The same Spirit is given to all of us. If God can make the entire universe merely by speaking it into existence, it is absurd to think he can't help you.

One way that he helps you is through other believers. So...

5) Get connected and plugged in with other young Christians who want to grow in the faith. You become like the people you surround yourself with, so choose your friends wisely. If you desire to be a man of God, then seek out and surround yourself with people who are men of God.

I understand the impact that friends have on young men. By the time I see them interacting, they have gone through the educational system together for years. Asking them to ditch their friends will seem absurd, but given the fact that we become like the people we surround ourselves with, think about the consequences of choosing worldly people as our intimates.

We can continue to live ungodly lives, marry ungodly women, and raise our children in an ungodly manner. Or, we can choose to start at the cross and surround ourselves with a great cloud of witnesses (Hebrews 12:1-3). Another one of my favorites is Proverbs 27:17, which says, "As iron sharpens iron, so one man sharpens another." If our friends are spiritually dull, we will be dulled. If they are spiritually sharp, they will sharpen us. Bottom line, if your friends are spiritually unhealthy, move on!

An obvious objection to this line of thought is that it is going to be hard to be good influences ourselves if we completely avoid other people. That is not what I am advocating. You don't have to abandon them (that would do them no good), but you should engage with them from a position of strength, with wisdom and discretion. In other words, engage them on your own terms.

Making up your mind to make good friends is especially critical for high school students who have just graduated and are about to transition to college. Such people are very vulnerable, because they will want to fit in. It is a very dangerous time. That's why it is important to figure out who you are and what you believe in *now*. Once you get to college, intentionally go out of your way to find like-minded Christians who are interested in growing with you at the cross and not the world.

6) When you get to college, stay rooted. Immediately find a local congregation rooted in Scripture.

7) Find the local Christian youth groups, Bible studies, and programs. Get involved. The longer you push it off, the more difficult it is going to be. Get involved immediately. InterVarsity, Ratio Christi, and Campus Crusade for Christ are excellent groups to help you stay rooted in your faith.

8) Related to number four: create an accountability partner. Find someone who will hold you accountable that you trust will do just that. After you create an accountability partner, get connected with a mentor, someone a bit older than you that is rooted in the faith and can appropriately lead you to and from the cross. It could even be your own father. Imagine that?

Every example that we have discussed comes down to whether we are rooted in Scripture or the world. Which way you go will have significant, practical, impacts on your spiritual health.

As I mentioned in a previous chapter, at one time I was convinced I was depressed. However, in hindsight, I concluded that I was simply lacking contentment and purpose. Then I learned how to control my thoughts. One of the most significant thoughts I had to continually drive home in my own mind was found in the aforementioned Galatians 1:10. Who was I trying to please? Man? Myself? Or God. Was I focused on His Gospel or my life? By knowing what the Scriptures said and then acting on what the Scriptures said, a change in attitude followed. My spiritual health improved.

I am going to walk you through steps on how to control your thoughts.

The four steps I am going to give you on how to control your thoughts primarily come from a book titled, *The Mind and the Brain.*[22] However, the steps can be found in a variety of forms in a variety of resources. You may prefer Mark Devine's *The Way of the Sea* as it is less intense than *The Mind and the Brain.*

I will provide you with these steps and resources assuming that you are reading Scripture and you are allowing Scripture to renew your mind.

Romans 12:2, and a host of other passages, make it obvious that when we fix our eyes on Jesus, He moves within us and flows out of us. Romans 12:2 states that we should not be conformed to the patterns of this world but be transformed by the renewing of our mind. Well, how do you renew your mind? You meditate on God's Word. You think on those things which align themselves with purpose of God. That has to be a starting point.

What does this look like in practical application? Here we go:

Let's use 'lust' for our example. It is a common problem, especially for men. The Scriptures, for obvious reasons, insist that we should not have lustful thoughts. But women are so beautiful! How can we resist such a temptation? Here are the four steps we use in class to assist us in maintaining those godly thoughts:

1. Recognize your thoughts
2. Question your thoughts
3. Replace your thoughts
4. Change your activity

All four of these steps take discipline. Creating new habits are difficult. Once you set your mind to meditating on God's Word daily and letting His Word work out His salvation through you, creating godly habits become easy because God is working in you.

---

[22] By Jeffery Schwartz.

Step 1: Recognize your thoughts.

This is easier said than done, isn't it? That's been one of the points throughout the book. A big part of our problem is that we are *not* recognizing our thoughts. We are being controlled by our worldly impulses because we have many unchallenged beliefs and thoughts. We have to develop our ability to monitor our own thinking.

As far as 'lust' goes, when we meditate on Scripture we will learn quickly what God thinks about it, and be confronted with our own thoughts. The contrast between God's thoughts and our thoughts will help us come to grips with our own life. However, this cannot be a one-time deal. Meditate on Scripture daily.

There you are, alone in your room with your phone or computer. An advertisement with a scantily clad girl pops up out of nowhere. Or, maybe a friend sends you a short video of a girl who is not dressed or is doing something provocatively. It only takes a quick look at an image to lead our thoughts astray.

What to do? We see the scantily dressed lady and we take "captive the thought."[23] We consciously recognize that we are about to, or are having a lustful thought. Now what?

Step 2: Question the thought.

Is this thought a thought you want in your brain? Is it a thought that is a godly thought? What does Scripture say about viewing this image? Is this a holy image or an unholy image? Again, this all takes discipline, but you have to start somewhere. God will help you. After you have rejected the thought as unhealthy, you have to move onto step three.

Step 3: Replace the thought.

Any time a lustful thought wants to find a safe space in my brain, I replace it with another thought. For me, that thought is, "This is not my wife. Think about your wife." From there, I continue doing whatever I was doing. The thought has been recognized, questioned, and replaced. I know it's not a thought I want because a lustful heart is not a godly or holy heart. I get that from Scripture. It is not always that easy and it will not be that easy for individuals who struggle

---

[23] 2 Corinthians 10:5

significantly with pornography or other lustful thoughts and activities. This brings us to step four.

Step 4: Change your behavior.

When men look at sexual images their brain reacts. Pornography is a huge industry because the people behind it know full well 1) how to trigger thoughts 2) that men are extremely visual and 3) that pornography is addictive. What happens with addiction is that the brain reacts to something pleasurable and wants to be rewarded with more pleasure.

It is a fight, but you must change your behavior! You must actually change what you are doing. You've recognized the thought, you've replaced the thought, now you must make a physical change. Sitting in your room alone having a mental fight with lustful thoughts is laudable, but it's unnecessary. Instead of staying in your room, *leave* the house and go for a walk, a run, a drive. Grab your phone and call a trusted friend and start having a conversation about homework. Sure, he will wonder why you have started caring about homework at 11pm, but you have changed your behavior and therefore have changed your thought.

It will be especially difficult at the beginning, and frankly never ceases to be a struggle to some degree, especially for men, but the more you do this, the easier it will become. The thing to remember is that thoughts can easily veer into action. If we lose control of our thoughts we can lose control of our actions.

Let's apply the process to another real world example:

You are at home with your girlfriend. You are downstairs on the couch, instead of upstairs with your parents. Both of you know that if the parents try to come downstairs, the steps will squeak, giving you an early warning of their presence. The two of you begin swapping saliva. Completely innocuous, right? (See previous chapters!) Let's be honest about it. The hormones are speaking and they are loudly encouraging you to continue beyond the kissing, if you know what I mean.

Step 1 Recognize the thought:

We *know* our hormones want to keep going, so we ought to be on our guard. If you have disciplined yourself to monitor your thought life, you will become aware of the fact that you have stopped thinking, and need to start thinking, right away!

Step 2: We question the thought.

Do I really want to be doing this with this girl? The hormones are screaming yes… but if you have been meditating on the Scriptures daily, you know the answer to that question.

Step 3 and Step 4: We replace the thought with a godly thought and we change our behavior.

You can bring the situation under control by something as simple as a comment to the effect that you respect her too much to go any further. You might add that you respect her parents, or your parents, or *her faith.* Wisdom says that having a discussion about it is probably not going to cut it, however. Remember the story of Joseph and Potiphar's wife![24] When she 'made herself available,' Joseph didn't stick around to have a rational conversation about the matter. He got out of dodge!

Change your behavior. Stand up. Go upstairs. Get a glass of water. Bring her with you. Sit down with your family or maybe go out to eat. Do something that makes it impossible for you to go too far sexually. (Ultimately, rather than playing with fire, may I recommend waiting for marriage before messing around at all?)

If you have been in such situations, you know that this is easier said than done. However, it is more than possible if you choose to start at the cross. God will help you.

The last example is yours to work through. I will give you the scenario and you can write down your process in the space provided. Recognize the thought, question the thought, replace it and change your behavior. Keep in mind that these steps are not timed. That said, in real life, after practicing the steps, it is not generally going to take you a long time to make a decision. It will become one fluid process.

Here is the scenario: your friends have convinced you to go to a party and you know some things about this particular event that leads you to conclude it will only bring trouble. You are sitting in your car contemplating the matter. Do you go, or not?

---

[24] Genesis 39.

Step 1:

Step 2:

Step 3:

Step 4:

This process of checking your thoughts and changing them is basic psychology.

Scientists have been encouraged by a new area of study called neuroplasticity. In short, neuroplasticity is a word used to describe the phenomena in which through your thoughts and actions you can literally change the physical structure of your brain.

Scientists used to think that once you were four or five years old, your brain structure was basically fixed in place. There was continued 'plasticity' until you were around twenty or so, but after that, the game was pretty much over. They thought that what was determined by that point pretty well dictated your thoughts and attitudes for the rest of your life.

Now the research shows that the more you think "x" thought, the more you are literally changing your brain, and it doesn't matter how old you are.[25] For example, if you keep telling yourself that you have no value or worth, it is not a mere thought. That thought will physically leave a 'mark' on your brain. You will be 'primed' to act on that thought, which in turn deepens the thought pattern that led to the action in the first place. Once the thought is 'burned' in like that, you will have to work your way out of it. To reverse it, you would need to change your thoughts, behaviors, and attitudes.

And, no lie, it is work. Yet, let us encourage each other with this *thought*: Whether it is lust, or depression, or greed and ambition, or gossiping, or... or... whatever it is, it is a choice. You have a choice to think a particular way. You have a choice to act in a certain way. You have a choice to accept God's help in making good choices. We are not forever enslaved to a certain way of thinking or doing things. By the power of the Holy Spirit, we *can* go another way.

Will you read the world into the Word,
or the Word into the world?

---

[25] It remains true, however, that the younger you are, the easier it is to change your brain by your thoughts. That speaks to how important it is to take control of your thought life now rather than wait. It also speaks to how important it is to raise your own children well, as it will be during their time with you that their brain will be most susceptible to influence.

Chapter 15

Why Did You Wake-Up Today?

There are many important questions that have been asked throughout this book. One of the most important questions that can help you on your way to becoming a godly man, one who oversees himself and his family appropriately, is posed in the title of this chapter.

When I talk to the freshmen on Prom Friday, the last question I ask them is, "Why did you wake up today?" Most students answer with the obligatory, "To come to school."

Ouch! I say. That has to be depressing. I ask them why their parents woke up. "To go to work?" they will gingerly ask. Bummer. If the only reason we are waking up on a daily basis is to scratch off items on a 'to do' list, it is no wonder life is so boring and tedious. I can see why students and teachers become depressed on Sunday night! They have to go back to school Monday only to suffer through to hump day and try to survive to Friday, only to repeat the count-down process the next week. If the only reason our parents woke up today was to punch numbers into a calculator and present a report the next day, I would be at my wit's end, too. The 'rat race' is never ending. Counting down days, weeks, or months, results in missed opportunities presented to you each and every day.

If you have not contemplated your own answer to this question, why not? What are you doing if you are not contemplating the complexities of life? Do you have something better to do? Are social media postings so important that we are ignoring one of the most important questions to ever be asked? When you answer this important question you will find meaning and purpose, and this in turn will spread into the other parts of your life, providing significance to activities and events that up to that moment you thought were mundane and boring. Your answer to our title's question is a game changer.

What is your purpose? Why did you wake up today?

The Christian and the atheist have conflicting and very different answers to these questions.

Atheists believes that there isn't a god. They believe there is no spiritual realm and that the universe as we know it is the result of an accidental instant explosion of matter and energy that did not exist.

When you take atheism to its logical conclusion, we are simply evolved animals living in a chance existence. The extent of your meaning and existence is literally no different than that of any other animal in the world. You are simply one link in the evolutionary chain.

The only value and meaning you have is what you or others give yourself. Having your value and purpose determined by your family, friends, and the world is depressing. If I am an atheist, then the reason I woke up today was to go to survive long enough to reproduce, nothing more, nothing less.

Some will argue that they are waking up so they can make a difference in the world. That's laudable, but nonetheless, it is not consistent with the atheistic worldview. If we are simply evolved animals doing what it takes to survive to advance ourselves and our family, why should we care about making a difference in a chance, chaotic, and literally meaningless world?

Unless of course, we actually do have value as humans and actually do have a real meaning and purpose which extends outside of ourselves. Then, it makes perfect sense that we might want to wake up and help improve the world. I would submit that the fact that few wish to live according to the nihilistic, but logically consistent, implications of atheism, is itself evidence that atheism is not true. Sure, people manage to ignore these contradictions and get about their lives, but if in fact there is a more coherent explanation that accounts for our dissatisfaction with the implications of atheism, one might be missing out on the proverbial 'meaning of life.'

Do you really think you exist because of pure accident? Do you really think that nothing existed and then out of nothing came something? Are you really going to say that you can rationally derive value, meaning and purpose, from chaotic circumstances? Get out. Get real. You know that you were meant to be here today, at this time, for these moments and opportunities. You know it. Perhaps you can't explain it, *but you know it.*

I can explain it. In my classes, I go into reasons for believing why Christianity is not merely reasonable and coherent, but actually true. That is not the purpose of this little book, however, so I will have to refer you to other sources to pick up that thread. For my purposes, I will take as my starting point the fact that you are very dissatisfied with the cold, purposeless existence that atheism says about us, and that you are eager for better news.

That better news: You woke up today because God has allowed you to wake up. If God exists, then He is responsible for the breath in your lungs today. You can try to argue that the alarm clock woke you up, but thousands of people die every year in their sleep. If that's the case, if you woke up because God allows you to wake up, then you woke up for an entirely different purpose than simply going to school.

Are you with me? You did not wake up to only go learn history or math, or to run the mile. You did not wake up to go to soccer practice. You did not wake up to try to make it to hump day. You woke up today to love God, to love people and to share His Gospel. *How* we do that differs according to our vocation as parents, teachers, students, athletes. The purpose is always the same. In everything we do, we do it for the glory of God.

In Matthew, Jesus says the two greatest commands are to, "Love the Lord your God with all your heart and with all your soul and with all your mind. This is the first and greatest commandment. And the second is like it: Love your neighbor as yourself."[26]

This is why *you* woke up today.

We carry out these 'commands' on the athletic fields, in the classrooms, punching numbers, predicting the weather, baking cupcakes, cleaning floors, cold calling people. It does not matter what you are doing or where you are at, when you are loving others, you are fulfilling your purpose of loving God.

You did not, however, wake up today to feel up your girlfriend, get drunk, flick someone off, cheat on a test, sleep in class, or disobey your parents. You woke up today to show honor and respect towards your girlfriend and to encourage your friends to do something else other than get drunk. Why? Because you love them and want the best for them. You woke up today to pay attention in class not because you want a good grade, but because in respecting your teacher you are loving your teacher and loving God at the same time. He has entrusted these teachers to you so that you may learn and grow. Likewise, teachers have been entrusted with students to help them learn and grow not only in content but primarily in life and faith. Moreover, by making the most of opportunities to improve your mind, you are showing respect for God, who made your mind.

If teachers are simply waking up to deliver you content, they are

---

[26] Matthew 22:37-39.

waking up for the wrong reasons. This is especially true of Christian teachers. When I was having my mental battle of contentment, I remember a veteran teacher making a bold statement in a faculty meeting. It was something to the effect of: If you are not here to love your students and put them first, then what are you doing? I was in a really bad spot back then and I cannot lie—I almost walked out. I was not invested, and I knew it. I was not answering that question appropriately. It is not always easy to love God and people in our daily life. Indeed, it can be a struggle. Nonetheless, the joy of living according to that purpose bears good fruit in the long term.

Becoming a godly man happens at the cross because we recognize that we need God! Becoming a godly man happens when Christ overcomes death and resurrects. Becoming a godly man happens when that same living and risen Christ, the Word, resides in you, making you a new creation.

This new creation is developed through the Word and reading His Word. When you answer the question, "Why did you wake up today" with the answer being, "To love God, love people, and share his Gospel," becoming a godly man becomes something *God* does through you.

Today is a gift. The breath in your lungs is a gift from the Creator of the universe. Today is not just another day, it is another opportunity. You have heard it said many times that you only get one shot at this life. Many times when you hear it, it is meant to encourage you to live life how you want, and make whatever choices you want, without having to worry about consequences. When people say that, they are just saying to "live it up."

Viewed from a Christian point of view though, God has created you to exist within this time in history with not a dictated existence but a purposed existence: One that knows him and shares his love with other people.

There are thousands of young men and women who were never given this opportunity because they were aborted. There are young men and women who have been given this opportunity to exist and have sadly chosen to end it too soon, were killed in tragic accidents, or died because of health issues. Adding to the tragedy, there are young men and women who are alive and well, wasting their opportunities. They view life as a drudgery, occasionally spiced up with pleasures and entertainment. They behave as though that is all there is to life. They live as though they can squander today's opportunities as though they have millions of days more, and can seize those opportunities later.

The real world is different. Setting aside the reality that lives are often cut short, the truth is that in the end, for all of us, the days will run out. Many of us are living ungrateful lives missing opportunities, benefits, and blessings given to us each day we are allowed to wake up. We have a roof over our head, food on our tables, warm water, an education, the ability to walk, read, sing, paint, throw, catch and breathe. We are sitting on a living lottery ticket with two options, to either sit on it at home, or to cash it in and make a difference for the Kingdom.

Life is a gift my, friend.

Today is another day and another opportunity, to love God, love people and to share His Gospel.

What are you waiting for?

Chapter 16

Living His Purpose

When you identify your purpose, your identity changes. When your identity changes and manifests itself outwardly, people notice.

In light of my newly grasped purpose, I am waking up to love God and to love people; I am letting people know that I belong to God. Why would I care about God's purpose for me if I don't identify as a child of God? If I don't belong to God then His purpose is pointless. One of the most important lessons a young Christian man can learn is that he does not belong to himself.

If God is responsible for the creation of the world then:

> The earth is the LORD's, and everything in it, the world, and all who live in it; for he founded it on the seas and established it on the waters. (Psalm 24:1).

You don't belong to yourself, you belong to God.

This unique relationship was created in the Garden when God created Adam and Eve. He made man in His special and unique image. Unfortunately, this unique image and relationship was destroyed with the fall of man. There was a gap separating man and God. God remained what he was—the most holy, pure and blameless entity that exists. Man became full of blame, impurities, and was unholy.

In case you didn't already know, God's holiness cannot coexist with our unholy selves.[27] God set out to solve this conundrum with

---

[27] If we put it the other way, it may be more comprehensible to you. We could say, "Radioactive materials cannot be close to people." Since radioactive materials don't care one bit what they are close to, it might be more accurate to say that people cannot be close to radioactive materials. The encounter will do great harm to the people, and nothing to the materials. To say this is not to render judgment, but simply to observe that the nature of humans is such that they don't respond well to exposure to uranium. Similarly, God is not at all 'harmed' by 'exposure' to a fallen creation. But, because of the nature of fallen creation, it cannot come into the presence of God—unless some accommodation is made. In the case of radioactive materials, humans can wear special suits and take other precautions. In the case of God, something more drastic was needed, which humans were incapable of achieving. So, God took the initiative and did the thing needful: made us holy again.

the death and sacrifice of Christ.

Paul makes mention of this in 1 Corinthians 6:19-20:

> Do you not know that your bodies are temples of the Holy Spirit, who is in you, whom you have received from God? You are not your own; you were bought at a price. Therefore honor God with your bodies.

As a young Christian man, you do not belong to yourself because God has purchased you with the blood of Christ. Through Christ we have our unique relationship and status with God again because when God views us, he doesn't see the corrupted image that was once perfectly complete in the Garden of Eden.

Instead, when God looks at us, He sees Christ who has restored the image of God to us through the cross. When we believe we belong to ourselves we undermine the authority of God. Why would I submit to God if I declare that I belong to myself? If I believe that I belong to myself, I undermine the very blood that Christ spilled to make me His.

This is why Paul said it didn't matter how awesome his education or lineage was. He understood that the most critical part of who he was is the fact that he belonged to Christ, the maker and creator of the world.

Through your own efforts, how much more valuable can you make yourself than being bought with the blood of God?

The life you live is the life entrusted to you by God. A steward is someone who takes care of the possessions of someone else. Pastors or Bible study leaders will speak about being wise stewards of the money entrusted to us by God. If the earth is the Lord's and everything in it, then the money we have is a blessing from God. It's not ours to be greedy with. Therefore, we should be wise stewards (caretakers) of the monetary blessings God has given us. Our 'possessions' on earth ultimately belong to God, and we are supposed to be wise stewards of these possessions. But it would be wrong to think that we are stewards only over material objects. As argued above, even our own body does not belong to ourselves, but rather to God. Likewise, the bodies of others belong to God.

A young lady does not belong to us; she has been entrusted to us by God. Our parents are not 'our' parents. They are the parents entrusted to us by God. The house that we live in is not our house. It is the house entrusted to us by God. My classroom is not "my" classroom, it is the classroom entrusted to me by God, which is loaded with students entrusted to me by God, to teach the students His truths and not my truths.

Understanding that we belong to God and not ourselves makes our purpose and perspective clear. If I belong to God and have been bought with God's blood, then why would I dishonor God's very blood by uniting it with a prostitute? If my girlfriend belongs to God and she has been bought with the blood of Christ, then why would I dishonor God's purchase by groping, fondling and making out with her?[28] The examples and implications are endless.

As a student, the teachers have been entrusted to you by God. Why would I dishonor the sacrifice of Christ's blood by being rude and disrespectful towards my teachers, parents, or coaches? They are a gift from God, entrusted to you, so that you may learn of His grace and truths. You do not belong to the teacher and the teacher does not belong to you. You both belong to God, therefore, honor one another appropriately.

This is a difficult truth and one that conflicts with a secular world which teaches you that you belong to yourself. You can do what you want, when you want, and with whomever you want, because it is your body. If it is your body, then it is your choice to do what you want with your body. "Who are you to judge me?" is often the question attached to this attitude. It is based off of the premise that we are our own authority. If I am my own authority, I submit to no one but myself. In short, I am declaring that I am my own god. But, if I'm a Christian, my authority is God. If my authority is God, then I submit to him.[29]

C. S. Lewis is one of the most notable Christian writers in history. Once an atheist, Lewis converted to Christianity. He wrote one of the best-selling pieces of Christian literature of all time, *The Screwtape Letters*. In this book, an elder demon is training his younger nephew

---

[28] Unless, of course, we were married. :) God does not forbid such behaviors. Rather, he provides a proper and appropriate context for those behaviors.

[29] It should go without saying that God's existence does not rise and fall based on whether or not people believe in him. Even people who don't believe in God still have God as the highest authority, even if they don't recognize it. However, my point here is that Christians themselves can fall into the trap of thinking, "My body, my choice." Of all people, they should understand who they belong to.

how to prevent and pull the Christian away from his faith. For the most part, each letter represents a different area of attack, different areas of vulnerability that the Christian is to be kept unaware of.

As an example, Screwtape (the elder uncle) encourages Wormwood (the younger nephew) to allow the Christian to maintain friendships, so long as the friendships are empty and without real substance. From their point of view, the demons are happy so long as the Christian is involved in anything unrelated to his faith. If his friends are keeping him preoccupied with fruitless conversations, all the better. The longer the Christian is oblivious to the negative influence of his friends, it's a win for them.

One of the most powerful letters in the entire book is Letter 21. Screwtape encourages Wormwood to convince his Christian that he belongs to himself. Wormwood is encouraged to persuade the Christian to believe that his time is his own. If the time belongs to the Christian, then the Christian can do whatever he wants with his time and his body.

It's one of the greatest lies that Christians buy into: they are the lone possessors of their body and the time they have on earth. In reality, as a Christian, we belong to God. Our bodies belong to God. The time which we have, right now, reading this book, belongs to God. The breath you just breathed belonged to God and therefore is a gift from him to you. This life you live is one entrusted to you by God to use for His glory and not for yours. The body of your girlfriend (or wife) is one entrusted to you by God to use for His glory and not for yours, or hers.

It is easy enough to see how our parents, spouses, children, etc. are not ours because they belong to God. Perhaps an unforeseen application of this truth is our interactions with strangers, people we don't know. They too, belong to God. That person that cut you off on the road, belongs to God. That referee that gave you a technical foul while you were sitting with the spectators? He belongs to God. That construction worker who is slowing your vacation down because of the road work he is doing, belongs to God.

As one who claims to be a Christian, this line of reasoning is inescapable. A godly man is one who belongs to God. He is one who recognizes that everything he has, actually isn't his, it belongs to God. We are God's stewards. We have been entrusted with life, with an opportunity to exist, to breathe, right here and right now. Misusing this gift is a slight against God and the free gift of salvation entrusted to you by God.

Being a godly man means being one who has given himself to the will of God in *all and every* aspect of this life entrusted to us by God.

It is our responsibility to make sure that we use this gift wisely, to love God, to love other people and to share His Gospel. After all, today is the day the Lord has made, let us rejoice and be glad in it (Psalm 118:24).

What will you do with *your* gift?

Chapter 17

You Are His VIP

Everyone wants to be a Very Important Person (VIP). It's engrained in our nature. If it is not engrained in our nature, it is certainly encouraged by our parents and educational and political systems. "It's all about *you!* Be whom you want, when you want! You are the best! Even if you are not the best, you are!" To put it differently, no one really wants to be a "loser." As much as I joke with my students that I do not care what they say about me, I don't want to go to work and be hated or not appreciated.

In much of this book, we have read about what it looks like to be a godly man or woman. Many of my personal failures were the result of my attempts to be important, whether it was socially, sexually, athletically, academically, spiritually, etc. I knew that academically I was not a genius. I certainly was not an academic VIP. Athletically, I had more gifts and talents and thus, I used those to bring myself status. I loved playing the games and competing, but the more I competed the more my identity was found in my athletic ability.

Worst of all, in my younger days, I would try to feel important by making others feel less important. Today, I cringe at what I did at the expense of others.

In elementary school, I walked from the back of the classroom to the front to grab a Kleenex. I then headed back towards my desk but not before stopping at one of my best friend's desks to give him a Kleenex to assist him while he was picking his nose. This was done, purposefully, in front of the entire class.

In high school, I once grabbed a kid's lunch tray and "politely" moved him to a different table because he was sitting at the senior table. Turns out, the kid was a newly transferred sophomore who was in his first days of school and literally had no idea what was going on. Ugh.

Embarrassing. Yet, despite my best efforts, my social currency never reached the millions. I was becoming morally bankrupt while having a social bank account with just a few thousand in it.

I was cool, but I was not the VIP.

I was a better athlete than many, but I was not the athletic VIP.

I went to a Christian school, but there was nothing about my family situation that gave me VIP status.

I would argue that today, more so than when I was growing up (just before the Internet became a thing), young men and women are seduced by the glamour of being a social, academic, athletic, or even spiritual VIP. We throw ourselves onto social media in hopes of getting a like or two, or three or four or five...We want the world to know who we are, what we look like and what we are doing! We want everyone to know we have arrived! We glorify and glamorize everyone and everything that should not be glorified. We want a piece of the action.

I had one student who wanted to move out to Hollywood so that she could become famous. When asked why she wanted to be famous the student responded, "I just want people to know me."

And we will do almost anything to be known, to be the VIP. In the process, we lose who Christ has called us to be: His.

You see, in Christ, we have a new VIP status. In Christ, our Value, Identity and Purpose all change. This is what I mean when I say that in all that we do, we start at the cross. We can fight tooth and nail to increase our social or monetary value, but at what cost? And when will we ever have enough to be satisfied?

What happens when our bank account is emptied because of having to pay child support or having to battle cancer? Does someone who is poor have less value than someone who is rich? Or what about someone who has no money at all? Are they valuable? Are they just as valuable as the pro basketball player making $32 million a year? If you listen to culture, the answer is yes. Yet if you listen to Scripture, it paints a different picture:

> But you are a chosen people, a royal priesthood, a holy nation, God's special possession, that you may declare the praises of him who called you out of darkness into his wonderful light. Once you were not a people, but now you are the people of God; once you had not received mercy, but now you have received mercy. (1 Peter 2:9-10)

In Christ, because of His mercy, you belong to God. You are His special possession. It doesn't matter how much money you have or don't have. It does not matter whether you are socially accepted or not. For those who are in Christ, you belong to God. You cannot get any more valuable than being purchased with the very blood of the Living God. What is more valuable than being redeemed by Christ himself?

Let's apply the same Scripture verse to your Identity. As an aging man, I have come to terms with the realization that athletically, I will not ever be where I used to be. For many years, my identity was found in my athletic ability. It certainly was not in my academic ability! If I was going to be known it was going to be through my athletics. I was not an academic. (That was my brother. He was the intellectual. I was the athlete.)[30]

Have you considered though what your identity looks like when you lose your athletic ability? When you can no longer out-run your players? Or your own children? What happens when the younger, more fit athletes show up at the rec center and wipe you and your game off the floor? In the first thirty seconds? *But I'm special because I am an athlete!* And if you are no longer an athlete? What then?

Age doesn't care. Neither does injury. If you have placed all of your stock in being an athlete and that is where your identity as a person lies, be ready for a surprise: It goes away. Quickly. Faster than the young rec players embarrassing you. Maybe it won't be age or injury that forces you to re-think your identity, but rather something else, trust me, if your identity is not rooted in God's view of you, life will eventually reveal how flimsy and unreliable it is.

For example, you might think your academics are what make you a stand out person. What happens if you go to a university where you discover that everyone has a higher SAT score than you?

When you no longer have your athletic or academic ability left, what happens of your identity? When we try to forge our own identity, we lose sight of the identity we have in Christ. We live by the world's standards as opposed to living as a redeemed child of God. If we belong to God, we are God's. We are his child. Homeless or millionaire. Professional athlete or washed-up theology teacher. We are His because of what He has done for us.

We have his Value and his identity. There isn't anything but a lack of belief that can take that away from you. And if we have his Value and his identity, we have his purpose. Life's greatest questions about who we are and what the "meaning of life" is, is answered at

---

[30] My brother would like it to be known that in his glory days, he was no slouch athletically, either. But *I* would like it to be noted, he was nothing compared to *me!*

the cross. You don't have to guess. You don't have to sacrifice yourself for the worldly pleasures because he has sacrificed himself for you.

Knowing that your VIP status is *His* Value, *His* Identity and *His* Purpose places us in less confusing and compromising position to live a godly life. A godly life that starts at the cross and stays at the cross.

And…leads others in the same direction.

> But if serving the Lord seems undesirable to you, then choose for yourselves this day whom you will serve, whether the gods your ancestors served beyond the Euphrates, or the gods of the Amorites, in whose land you are living. But as for me and my household, we will serve the Lord.
>
> Joshua 24:15

What are you willing to give up
to start and stay at the cross?

Appendix A

If you have made it this far I encourage you to go a little further. It will be worth your time. What follows below is a classic writing called, *A Message to Garcia*, written and published by Elbert Hubbard in 1899.[31] Until recently, it has been a staple of the United States Marine Corps reading list. When we talk about what a godly man looks like, we are talking about a man who gets the job done, correctly and with integrity. A man is someone who accomplishes the task without making excuses or complaining. A man is someone who sees a task and completes the task without even having to be asked to do it. You never have to ask *a man* to do the right thing.

In the context of this book, we need godly men and women who will start at the cross and lead their families without making excuses, complaining or waiting to be asked to do what needs to be done. We need people of integrity and service.

Hubbard provides us with an example of such a person: Rowan. Rowan has been summoned to deliver a message to Garcia. His task? Find out in the full text of Hubbard's essay, below.

Bottom line: *Get it done.*

A Message to Garcia

> In all this Cuban business there is one man stands out on the horizon of my memory like Mars at perihelion. When war broke out between Spain and the United States, it was very necessary to communicate quickly with the leader of the Insurgents. Garcia was somewhere in the mountain fastnesses of Cuba — no one knew where. No mail or telegraph could reach him. The President must secure his co-operation, and quickly. What to do! Someone said to the President, "There's a fellow by the name of Rowan will find Garcia for you, if anybody can."
>
> Rowan was sent for and given a letter to be delivered

[31] ISBN: 978-1947844179

to Garcia. How "the fellow by name of Rowan" took the letter, sealed it up in an oil-skin pouch, strapped it over his heart, in four days landed by night off the coast of Cuba from an open boat, disappeared into the jungle, and in three weeks came out on the other side of the island, having traversed a hostile country on foot, and having delivered his letter to Garcia, are things I have no special desire now to tell in detail.

The point I wish to make is this: McKinley gave Rowan a letter to be delivered to Garcia; Rowan took the letter and did not ask, "Where is he at?" By the Eternal! There is a man whose form should be cast in deathless bronze and the statue placed in every college in the land. It is not book-learning young men need, nor instruction about this or that, but a stiffening of the vertebrae which will cause them to be loyal to a trust, to act promptly, concentrate their energies; do the thing — "carry a message to Garcia!" General Garcia is dead now, but there are other Garcias.

No man, who has endeavored to carry out an enterprise where many hands were needed, but has been well-nigh appalled at times by the imbecility of the average man — the inability or unwillingness to concentrate on a thing and do it. Slipshod assistance, foolish inattention, dowdy indifference, and half-hearted work seem the rule; and no man succeeds, unless by hook or crook, or threat, he forces or bribes other men to assist him; or mayhap, God in His goodness performs a miracle, and sends him an Angel of Light for an assistant.

You, reader, put this matter to a test: You are sitting now in your office—six clerks are within your call. Summon any one and make this request: "Please look in the encyclopedia and make a brief memorandum for me concerning the life of Corregio."

Will the clerk quietly say, "Yes, sir," and go do the task?

On your life, he will not. He will look at you out of a fishy eye, and ask one or more of the following questions:

Who was he?
Which encyclopedia?
Where is the encyclopedia?
Was I hired for that?
Don't you mean Bismarck?
What's the matter with Charlie doing it? Is he dead?
Is there any hurry?
Shan't I bring you the book and let you look it up yourself?
What do you want to know for?

And I will lay you ten to one that after you have answered the questions, and explained how to find the information, and why you want it, the clerk will go off and get one of the 2 other clerks to help him find Garcia — and then come back and tell you there is no such man. Of course I may lose my bet, but according to the Law of Average, I will not. Now if you are wise you will not bother to explain to your "assistant" that Corregio is indexed under the C's, not in the K's, but you will smile sweetly and say, "Never mind," and go look it up yourself.

And this incapacity for independent action, this moral stupidity, this infirmity of the will, this unwillingness to cheerfully catch hold and lift, are the things that put pure socialism so far into the future. If men will not act for themselves, what will they do when the benefit of their effort is for all? A first mate with knotted club seems necessary; and the dread of getting "the bounce" Saturday night holds many a worker in his place. Advertise for a stenographer, and nine times out of ten who apply can neither spell nor punctuate — and do not think it necessary to.

Can such a one write a letter to Garcia? "You see that bookkeeper," said the foreman to me in a large factory. "Yes, what about him?" "Well, he's a fine accountant, but if I'd send him to town on an errand, he might accomplish the errand all right, and, on the other hand, might stop at four saloons on the way, and when he got to Main Street, would forget what he had been sent for."

Can such a man be entrusted to carry a message to Garcia? We have recently been hearing much maudlin sympathy expressed for the "down-trodden denizen of the sweat shop" and the "homeless wanderer searching for honest employment," and with it all often go many hard words for the men in power.

Nothing is said about the employer who grows old before his time in a vain attempt to get frowsy ne'er-do-wells to do intelligent work; and his long patient striving with "help" that does nothing but loaf when his back is turned. In every store and factory there is a constant weeding-out process going on. The employer is constantly sending away "help" that have shown their incapacity to further the interests of the business, and others are being taken on. No matter how good times are, this sorting continues, only if times are hard and work is scarce, this sorting is done finer - but out and forever out, the incompetent and unworthy go. It is the survival of the fittest. self-interest prompts every employer to keep the best-those who can carry a message to Garcia.

I know one man of really brilliant parts who has not the ability to manage a business of his own, and yet who is absolutely worthless to anyone else, because he carries with him constantly the insane suspicion that his employer is oppressing, or intending to oppress, him. He can not give orders, and he will not receive them. Should a message be given him to take to Garcia, his answer would probably be, "Take it yourself."

Tonight this man walks the streets looking for work, the wind whistling through his threadbare coat. No one who knows him dare employ him, for he is a regular firebrand of discontent. He is impervious to reason, and the only thing that can impress him is the toe of a thick-soled No. 9 boot. Of course I know that one so morally deformed is no less to be pitied than a physical cripple; but in your pitying, let us drop a tear, too, for the men who are striving to carry on a great enterprise, whose working hours are not limited by the whistle, and whose hair is fast turning white through the struggle to hold the line in dowdy indifference, slipshod imbecility, and the heartless ingratitude which, but for their enterprise, would be both hungry and homeless.

Have I put the matter too strongly? Possibly I have; but when all the world has gone a-slumming I wish to speak a word of sympathy for the man who succeeds — the man who, against great odds, has directed the efforts of others, and, having succeeded, finds there's nothing in it: nothing but bare board and clothes. I have carried a dinner-pail and worked for a day's wages, and I have also been an employer of labor, and I know there is something to be said on both sides. There is no excellence, per se, in poverty; rags are no recommendation; and all employers are not rapacious and high-handed, any more than all poor men are virtuous.

My heart goes out to the man who does his work when the "boss" is away, as well as when he is home. And the man who, when given a letter for Garcia, quietly takes the missive, without asking any idiotic questions, and with no lurking intention of chucking it into the nearest sewer, or of doing aught else but deliver it, never gets "laid off," nor has to go on strike for higher wages. Civilization is one long anxious search for just such individuals. Anything such a man asks will be granted; his kind is so rare that no employer can afford to let him go. He is wanted in every city, town, and village — in every office, shop, store and factory. The world cries out for such; he is needed, and needed badly—the man who can Carry a message to Garcia.

Are you the kind of person who makes excuses, who asks questions for the sake of asking questions? Do you find others to do to the work you have been assigned to do because you are too lazy? Copy off others in school? Hid in the back room while others worked? This classic reading is a call to arms to men to be men: to lead and get the job done.

1 Timothy 3 is a call to overseers to be above reproach. A call to lead and conduct oneself worthy of the calling of being a disciple of Christ. Christ has given you a message to deliver. A message of hope.

The Message of the Gospel.

Deliver the message in a way that is:

> ...above reproach, faithful to his wife, temperate, self-controlled, respectable, hospitable, able to teach, not given to drunkenness, not violent but gentle, not quarrelsome, not a lover of money.

"Love God, love people, share the Gospel.
That's how you get it done."

Delainee Wheeler

Appendix B

Links for Skeptic.com's article on pornography:

Original Article: http://www.skeptic.com/reading_room/how-porn-is-messing-with-your-manhood/
Response article: http://www.skeptic.com/reading_room/guard-your-manhood-response-to-marty-klein/

Links the author used in the paragraph cited in this book:

http://www.ncbi.nlm.nih.gov/pubmed/25032736
http://www.ncbi.nlm.nih.gov/pubmed/25032736
http://journals.plos.org/plosone/article?id=10.1371/journal.pone.0102419
http://onlinelibrary.wiley.com/doi/10.1111/j.1559-1816.1988.tb00027.x/abstract
http://www.ncbi.nlm.nih.gov/pubmed/25189834
http://www.ncbi.nlm.nih.gov/pubmed/18343988
http://www.ncbi.nlm.nih.gov/pubmed/25466233
http://link.springer.com/article/10.1007%2Fs11199-012-0164-0
http://www.ncbi.nlm.nih.gov/pubmed/22449010
http://www.ncbi.nlm.nih.gov/pubmed/21259151
http://www.ncbi.nlm.nih.gov/pmc/articles/PMC2891580/
http://onlinelibrary.wiley.com/doi/10.1111/j.1475-6811.2010.01328.x/abstract
http://onlinelibrary.wiley.com/doi/10.1111/j.1559-1816.1988.tb00027.x/abstract
http://www.tandfonline.com/doi/abs/10.1080/19317611.2014.927048#.V2C8m_krLIU
http://www.tandfonline.com/doi/abs/10.1080/19317611.2014.927048

Appendix C

Important questions for reflection addressed in *UnConformed:*

1. What does a godly man or woman look like?
2. Who am I?
3. What do I actually believe?
4. What does my belief look like manifested in my daily existence?
5. Why is judging someone's actions and holding those actions up to Scripture important for leading yourself and your family towards the cross?
6. Are you heading away or towards the cross of Christ?
7. If you are not who you are supposed to be, then who are you meant to be?
8. How do your currently established patterns echo into the future?
9. Are you leading others away or towards Christ?
10. What do others say about you? And is it true?
11. When someone looks at you, who do they see? You or Christ's holiness?
12. Will your son lead their wives and children towards Christ or away from him?
13. Are you standing vigilant against the hollow and deceptive philosophies of the world?
14. Who is in control? You or your emotions?
15. Are you respectful because that's what you are supposed to do, or because you *are* respect? Honor? Integrity?
16. Will you live selfishly or love selflessly?
17. What are you teaching your siblings, significant other, spouse or children by your actions?
18. What pattern will you create that your children and their children will follow?
19. What do you listen to and watch that not only influences who you are, but bleeds into the lives of others?
20. Exactly how will you do what you have been called to do?

21. What's more important to you? — Social and monetary currency, or being rich in Christ?
22. Are you reading the world into the Word, or the Word into the world?
23. Why did you wake up today?
24. What are you waiting for?
25. Are you living *his* purpose or your own?
26. What are the consequences of living your own purpose as opposed to his purpose?
27. What will you do with your gift of life?
28. What are you willing to give up to start and stay at the cross?
29. Where do you find identity? In yourself, or in *his* identity as your savior?
30. Is your value found in the world and yourself, or in the very blood and holiness of Christ himself?
31. What, or who, determines "your" VIP status?
32. Who or what are you willing to sacrifice to increase your social currency?

55675670R00090

Made in the USA
Columbia, SC
17 April 2019